REINVENTING
INFLUENCE

REINVENTING
INFLUENCE

how to get things
done in a world
without authority

Mary Bragg

London · Hong Kong · Johannesburg
Melbourne · Singapore · Washington DC

PITMAN PUBLISHING
128 Long Acre, London WC2E 9AN
Tel: +44 (0)171 447 2000
Fax: +44 (0)171 240 5771

A Division of Pearson Professional Limited

First published in Great Britain 1996

ISBN 0 273 62313 3

British Library Cataloguing in Publication Data
A CIP catalogue record for this book can be obtained from the British Library.

10 9 8 7 6 5 4 3 2 1

Typeset by Northern Phototypesetting Co Ltd, Bolton
Printed and bound in Great Britain by Bell & Bain Ltd, Glasgow

The Publishers' policy is to use paper manufactured from sustainable forests.

about the author

Mary Bragg worked for the multinational, Glaxo-Wellcome, before undertaking a range of consultancy projects in Human Resource Management when seconded to Coopers & Lybrand, both in the UK and internationally. Her professional qualifications include a Masters Degree in Organisational Behaviour. She is currently a Principal Lecturer in the Faculty of Business at London Guildhall University. As an independent management consultant, she runs external and in-company courses on *"Reinventing Influence,"* further information on which can be obtained from Mary Bragg, PO Box 10248, London SW20 8ZF, UK.

To Andrew and Peggy,
the key influences in my life

acknowledgments

To research and then write this book, certain influential people have allowed me to follow my dreams and to indulge "a proper selfishness."

To my husband, my mother, and my brother, therefore, I offer my unreserved thanks.

I acknowledge my debt to Laura, whose transformation from an "organizational hermit" into a master influencer is the true inspiration behind the title.

I thank my friend and colleague, Professor Eugene McKenna, for his encouragement of my research into business skills development.

I also thank my commissioning editor, Victoria Siddle, who was so inspired by the power of influence as to make *Reinventing Influence* possible.

contents

chapter six

STEP FOUR – DECIDE ON STRATEGY AND TACTICS   179

chapter seven

THE ROAD TO MASTERY   213

introduction

How do you cope when subordinates are unwilling to accept military-style orders? Or when you suddenly find yourself managing an international team of experts over whom you have no direct authority? Or when you must sell a proposal which can only be justified by the numbers, to a boss who hates numbers? In the modern world of work, none of these circumstances is unusual.

The world is currently experiencing possibly its biggest ever business revolution. Managers in every field – in the private and public sectors, in services and manufacturing – are being forced to rethink the management principles which have guided their institutions for so long. The old certainties are gone. The old hierarchical structures with their antiquated command and control systems – all heavily promoted in the last quarter of a century – are now on the scrap heap of corporate history.

That is not to say that such structures and systems did not make sense in their day, quite the reverse. But today's business world has lost its orderly and predictable stability; today's employees have a different attitude toward authoritarian structures, and life has lost its security. Increasing global competition, the constant need for innovation, together with rapid and unpredictable changes in business methods, have all seen to that.

Systems and procedures stifle managers' ability to thrive in the new chaotic order. They simply have not got the time to write those long numbers-driven reports, which go up and down the corporate hierarchy for never ending review and consideration. Things are changing too rapidly – such iterated analysis runs the risk of being out-of-date before it finally hits the CEO's desk.

> The world is currently experiencing possibly its biggest ever business revolution. Managers in every field are being forced to rethink the management principles which have guided their institutions for so long.

The new order drives us away from an excessive concern with data and balance sheets back toward the softer skills of vision, values, networks, negotiation, self-presentation, and culture. In other words, all those skills that we need in order to work with and through people to get results in a turbulent and chaotic world.

Ironically, our technology-driven age puts a premium on the basic, centuries-old common sense skills which guided the founding fathers of business. The lack of systems, procedures, and human resource management schemes did not hinder their entrepreneurial endeavors. They had something better. They had an intuitive feel for how to work with people. They knew how to build networks, exchange favors, talk to their customers, negotiate finance in the coffee houses of London, and make upward appeals to those in higher authority. Our business forefathers exploited to the full the whole host of interpersonal and social skills which modern managers now need to reinvent in order to unleash the power resources available to them.

What differentiates today's situation, however, from that of our forefathers is the sheer extent to which we need to be able to exercise influence, in other words, the scale of today's interdependence. Not only was the number of companies in existence significantly lower in the nineteenth century, compared to today, those companies also employed fewer people. In addition, the scope of those nineteenth-century businesses would have been much less extensive – the constraints of the communication and transportation systems, for example, would have limited the geographical range of consumers and suppliers alike.

> Ironically, our technology-driven age puts a premium on the basic, centuries-old common sense skills which guided the founding fathers of business. The lack of systems, procedures, and human resource management schemes did not hinder their entrepreneurial endeavors. They had something better.

Things are different now. Markets are global; product and service delivery systems are sophisticated enough to deliver "mass customization"; communication systems bind the world together in real time; scattered workforces are sited in areas of lowest cost; and the old corporate vertical pyramids have been deconstructed. This means that you as a manager may be dependent on literally hundreds, possibly thousands, of different people to get things done. And not only will there be this inter-dependence with a mind-boggling number of potential business partners, in all probability, you will exercise no direct authority or power over them whatsoever.

This places a premium on the ability to build effective and influential relationships with the most unfamiliar and alien of people. Steven Spielberg's film *ET* pro-vides a parable: the rational scientists descend on the Extra Terrestrial with their checklists and sophisticated analytical techniques, and almost suc-ceed in measuring ET to death. In contrast, the chil-dren reach out to ET on an emotional level and receive as their reward a vision beyond their dreams. The parable tells us that we all respond to and are influenced by people who are able to reach us emotionally.

> All the top-notch people you will meet throughout this book share a huge capacity to wield influence and reach people to achieve results in their particular fields of activity.

Consider the true, though larger-than-life example of Tony O'Reilly, who excelled at Rugby Union football for not only Ire-land but also the rampaging British Lions, before developing a meteoric business career which has taken him to the top of the Heinz Corporation in the United States. One of the key skills for which he has always been noted is the ability to build immediate relationships with anyone: from the humblest Irish farmer or South African rugby veteran, to world presidents and statesmen, all of whom he can work through and influence. Not for nothing did Henry Kissinger dub O'Reilly a "Renaissance Man," highly appropriate for an individual who has truly reinvented influence.

All the top-notch people you will meet throughout this book share this huge capacity to be able to wield influence and reach people to achieve results in their particular fields of activity. It may be Bob Geldof, mobilizing generations of young and old across the world for *Band Aid*; or Nelson Mandela, uniting the spirit of an entire nation by the massively simple act of appearing at the final of the 1995 Rugby Union World Cup wearing the

South African team shirt bearing the number of the revered white captain; or John Sculley, communicating his inspirational vision at Apple Computers. In their different ways, all are modern masters of the ancient skill of exercising influence.

The changes introduced by the white-heat of technology have made management into a white-knuckle, roller coaster ride, where you must learn to master the art of being on the brink of control. Riding the horses on the merry-go-round was predictable and safe, but unfortunately, it is no longer an available option. So, join me on the management roller coaster as we learn how to thrive on the chaos of this global management revolution.

The challenges ahead are not for the faint-hearted: they demand courage and the ability to dream new possibilities. They ask the manager to leave behind the world of the organizational hermit where a memo is sent to a peer and copied to the boss (though "for information only", of course) rather than mastering a difficult face-to-face meeting. To be effective, a manager must throw away this crutch of authority and stand on his own two feet by rediscovering people and getting things done through influence.

■ The roller coaster ahead

As you speed along the roller coaster, you will have the opportunity to throw away all those sure-fire management guides dedicated to analytical, business rationality, which promised universal management success. You must now concentrate on rediscovering yourself and other people.

The first challenge in chapter one will be to consider why influence skills have become central to the repertoire of skills needed by the manager in modern organizations. This part of the ride will turn you upside down – are you holding on?

Our roller coaster will then take you into alien territory – the six psychological principles of influence and how you can use them to activate the seven power levers at your disposal in organizational life. Knowledge is power; and the more knowledge you have of the psychological processes underpinning how to influence your target, the more successful you will be.

The ride then accelerates into the emotionally disturbing land of the "touchy-feely" – there is not a single figure, or rational argument in sight! Can you cope?

Chapter two asks you to focus on the need to understand yourself before you can use influence effectively. Beliefs, values, and assumptions all have an impact on your success in influencing others to secure commitment to your goals. The chapter stresses the need to consciously manage them in order to control the impressions you create with the people whom you need to influence. Not going too fast?

Mind-boggling degrees of interdependence mean that you must learn to identify your potential target successfully. This is a difficult task, but an essential skill to avoid falling off the roller coaster – chapter four shows you how.

All journeys involve learning about cultures, heroes, myths, stories, rituals, tribal customs, and networks. Our roller coaster ride is no exception – we too must discover the hidden informal cultures and networks which hold today's flat, interdependent organizations together and we must find out what kinds of influencing behavior are acceptable.

Every journey must have a goal. Our journey nears its conclusion in chapter six by looking at influence strategy – are strong strategies more effective than soft strategies? Not only does the chapter demonstrate that soft strategies are the preferred choice; it swoops down into the detail of the eight tactical weapons of influence. After all, understanding strategy is no use unless you understand the tactics too!

Chapter seven reviews the roller coaster ride of reinventing influence which we have enjoyed together. Just as importantly, it prepares you to go on the white-knuckle ride on your own, by showing you how to put into effective practice the ideas presented during our journey.

■ You are not alone

On the roller coaster ride, you will see many top-flight people racing around the track ahead of you. All of them spirited, all of them interesting, they boast a wide variety of backgrounds, from finance to football, politics to production, arts to airlines, right around the globe. The names to look out for as they shoot by include:

Jack Welch, chairman and CEO of General Electric (one of the world's largest corporations) who is attempting to transform the century-old giant into a totally network-based organization.

John Sculley, whose experience includes time at Pepsico and Apple Computers (chairman and CEO).

John DeLorean, brash young executive at General Motors who went on to head Pontiac, Chevrolet and his own DeLorean Motor Company in Northern Ireland.

Rupert Murdoch, global communications magnate.

Robert Maxwell, who went from Eastern European immigrant to controversial global media tycoon.

Bill Clinton, president of the United States of America.

Boris Yeltsin, president of Russia.

Alan Sugar, chairman of Amstrad and of Tottenham Hotspur Football Club.

Tony Blair, former lawyer and now leader of the British Labour Party.

Michael Heseltine, magazine proprietor and deputy prime minister of the United Kingdom.

Lawrence A. Bossidy, chairman and CEO of Allied Signal, the $13 billion turnover supplier of aerospace systems, automotive parts, and chemical products.

Richard Branson, creator of the world-renowned Virgin empire, stretching from music to airlines via finance.

Margaret Thatcher, former UK prime minister, one of the most influential women of our times.

Anita Roddick, cofounder and CEO of the Body Shop.

Bill Gates, chairman and CEO of the Microsoft organization.

Steve Jobs, cofounder and long-time chairman and technical leader of Apple Computers.

Kelvin MacKenzie, one-time editor of the best-selling UK tabloid newspaper – *The Sun*.

Tiny Rowland, multimillionaire merchant adventurer, former chairman and chief executive of the Lonrho empire.

Hillary Clinton, the current First Lady of the American White House, and former US lawyer.

Richard Goodwin, former president and CEO of Johns-Manville, Inc.

Tony Berry, former chairman of Blue Arrow plc, the largest employment agency in the world.

Henry Kissinger, consultant to President Kennedy, special assistant for national security affairs in the first Nixon administration.

Harold Geneen, former CEO of ITT.

James Hanson, eponymous head of the multimillion-pound Hanson empire.

Ross Johnson, the former chief executive of R.J.R. Nabisco.

Peter McClough, former chief executive of the Xerox Corporation.

And Laura, the heroine of the various episodes in our feature case study found at the end of each chapter. This case study fictional-izes events at a real company, which is British-based but Ameri-can-owned. Laura is a real person with whom I worked as she traveled the difficult journey to reinventing influence.

When I first met her, she was utterly typical of the cerebral, analysis-oriented managers who graduate from our MBA courses – more as masters of administration, perhaps, than of business. Although she was undoubtedly one of the brightest and best, her inability to use influence effectively impeded her professional progress.

Laura should be the inspiration to all managers reading this book. In spite of, and probably because of, the toe-curling mis-takes, the tough challenges, the unremitting self-examination, the continual unlearning and relearning she endured, she came out as a top-level influencer and performer. I urge you to use Laura's example to stay the course.

> When I first met Laura she was utterly typical of the cerebral, analysis-oriented managers who graduate from our MBA courses – more as masters of administration, perhaps, than of business.

So let's make a start. Take your last opportunity before the roller coaster moves off to wave goodbye to the dead and lonely world of those timid grey souls who know neither victory nor defeat. Tense your knuckles as the speeds picks up – shout and scream if you must – but hang on – the world belongs to you if you can learn how to reinvent the skills of influence.

Mary Bragg, 1996

key to symbols

The following symbols are used throughout this book to help the reader.

 Self-assessment exercise / action checklist.

 A definition.

 Recent findings.

 Concept quiz.

 Feature case study.

 Summary checklist.

 Quote

A CHANGING WORLD

This chapter examines the relationship between influence skills and managerial effectiveness. It looks at the changing nature of organizations in the 1990s and the subsequent impact on the nature of the manager's role. The chapter also highlights how influence skills have become central to the repertoire of techniques and strategies needed by managers.

SELF-ASSESSMENT EXERCISE

Are you using influence effectively?

Complete the following questions to identify some of the problems you encounter in influencing others at work:

1. List all those people you work directly with or through.

_____

_____

2. List those people in the organization whom it may be useful to know.

_____

_____

3. List the major tasks you do at work.

_____

_____

4. Estimate the proportion of time you spend between the following:

   (a) building relationships,

   (b) completing your major tasks,

   (c) attending formal meetings.

_____

_____

5. What are the main problems you encounter in seeking to influence others at work?

_____

_____

Follow-up

It is most likely that you are spending the majority of your time either just getting your tasks done or attending formal meetings. In these formal meetings, you will tend to rely on logical analysis to persuade others that your particular project or proposal is the only correct way forward.

Typically, you will devote very little attention or time to developing the network of people with whom you come into direct contact while working. Nor, typically, will you pay much attention to the people with whom you are not in regular direct contact, but who might in fact be very useful to know.

You would be unusual if you did not encounter problems in getting the decisions you want – reasons might include:

- a failure to take the audience with you,
- wrongly assuming that the key players all shared identical goals,
- ignoring "emotional" reactions to proposals,
- forgetting that men and women *are* irrational,
- trying too hard,
- having no knowledge of others' "hidden agendas,"
- underestimating the political dimensions of organizational life.

In sum, you are probably forgetting the power and importance that the skills of influence have in modern organizational life.

The manager and influence

One of the most significant and undervalued managerial skills is the ability to influence others. Ask any manager and he or she will tell you that simply doing a good job is just not enough. Managers recognize that in addition, they must be able to change other people's attitudes to events, people, and decisions through their interpersonal and social skills. These skills include personal negotiation, getting on with people, fitting in, understanding other people's motives and goals, self-presentation, and so on. Influence has an impact on absolutely every aspect of managerial work.

Recent research by Henry Mintzberg has exploded the stereotype of the manager as a reflective planner.[1] It appears that most managers shun formal reports, skim periodicals, and merely process mail. Indeed, Gabarro has shown that many managers boast that their primary objective is to "get the monkey off their backs" and onto the backs of others with as much speed and with as little personal intervention as possible.[2]

The everyday reality as revealed by Mintzberg is that most managers prefer to gather information from meetings or telephone calls and that they rely heavily on gossip and hearsay, both inside and outside the company, to keep up-to-date.[3] They make agreements during chance encounters in corridors, and they form impressions and judgments about peers, subordinates, and superiors alike on a very narrow range of interpersonal cues. These cues typically include style of dress, accent, gender, age, and so on. It does not matter whether the meetings are in the conference room or corridor, success still depends on a high degree of interpersonal and social influence.

Since his original research on the nature of managerial work, Mintzberg has been deluged by letters from managers relieved to find that the stereotypical manager – utterly rational, utterly cerebral – really was a myth. The following extract is typical:

"You make me feel so good. I thought all those other managers were planning, organizing, co-ordinating and controlling, while I was busy being interrupted, jumping from one issue to another, and trying to keep the lid on the chaos."[4]

In subsequent research on successful chief executives, Mintzberg discovered that they too tend to favor the insightful/intuitive aspects of their activities rather than the cerebral/analytical.[5] Their success was rooted in their ability to handle ambiguity, inconsistency and chaos, areas where forging interpersonal connec-tions and exercising influence were paramount. In contrast, those managers who favored analysis and diligence were sucked down into the quagmire of closely typed reports and energy-sapping paperwork. Their ideas, often highly creative and laudable, tended to be left behind. The real mistake of these diligent, analysis-led managers was to ignore the vital interpersonal connections and the hidden, often infor-mal, links which lie beneath the surface of every organization.

Mintzberg has been deluged by letters from managers relieved to find that the stereotypical manager – utterly rational, utterly cerebral – really was a myth.

The ability to influence others is a vital component, therefore, of managerial effectiveness and success. Obviously it is not the only component. Mintzberg argues that in practice, successful management lies in balancing two complementary factors: the cerebral *and* the insightful.[6] This means that managers must be content-oriented, as well as process-/skills-oriented. Either com-ponent on its own will not produce an effective manager. Cere-bral managers will remain socially and organizationally inept, while "streetwise," but otherwise unqualified, managers will be constrained by the limits of their technical competence.

It follows, therefore, that the training of business managers should pay equal importance to these two aspects – the cognitive and insightful. This parallels the situation in medicine, where trainee doctors receive training in interpersonal skills ("bedside manner") to ensure that their technical/diagnostic skills are fully utilized.

In business, this means that training should focus not only on cognitive learning in disciplines such as accountancy, marketing, law, and economics (which currently form the basis of most of our business and management education). Training should also focus on the insightful, the so-called softer skills such as personal negotiation, getting on with people, motivating, networking, and developing allies.

It is questionable how much importance business and management schools attach to the softer skills of influence, concentrating their teaching efforts more on analysis at the expense of personal skills. Is it purely a coincidence that Germany and Japan, two of the strongest industrial nations over the last 50 years, boast a very low number of business schools?

> The training of business managers should pay equal importance to these two aspects – the cognitive and insightful.

The controversy surrounding the MBA degree illustrates the dangers of not achieving a balance between the two factors. Various studies have suggested that the investment in the MBA degree may pay off for the individual participant, but that there is little evidence of how such education has increased the value of the business corporations to which they return.[7] Some believe that the best managers have no MBA – it is certainly true that many successful entrepreneurs have made it without the benefit of a University education – Richard Branson, founder of the Virgin empire, for example. Similarly, Bill Gates went on leave from Harvard College at the age of 19 in order to start the now world-famous Microsoft company.

This argument is supported by Ian Campbell Bradley, who, when discussing "historical entrepreneurs," suggests that it was something other than education which was responsible for their entrepreneurial activity.[8]

Many companies are now sceptical of MBA graduates, whom they perceive as possessing the cognitive knowledge, but lacking in interpersonal skills to make that knowledge effective – the skills of gaining others' commitment and support, for example. When MBA graduates first enter a company, they tend to be swamped by political intrigue, feuds, and hidden cultural values and secrets, while they try to swim with their newly acquired technical skills. Such ineptitude usually results in frustration, and sometimes in drowning.

In summary, any modern successful manager must balance the insightful and cerebral. This means being able to interpret a political situation as easily and as correctly as a balance sheet. The inability to achieve this balance represents a wasted opportunity.

The need for influence

There is nothing new about the need for influence skills. As early as the third century BC, the Indian, Kautilya, recognized the significance which influence has over power in the art of statecraft. The contribution of the fifteenth-century Florentine statesman, Niccolo Machiavelli, to the art of using influence has been so great (in *The Prince*,[9] for example) that his name has entered the English language as a byword for self-interested, political intrigue and machination:

> "Princes who have achieved great things have been those who have given their word lightly, who have known how to trick men with their cunning, and who, in the end, have overcome those abiding by honest principles."[9]

Nineteenth-century managers and executives were fairly indistinguishable from modern-day counterparts. Although the types of information and technology they used were obviously different, the need to exercise influence was as important then as it is now, whether collecting information by word of mouth, networking, or linking into rumors and whispers.

What is crucially different for twentieth-century managers compared to their forebears, however, is the sheer extent to which they must be able to exercise influence. Now more than ever before, influence rather than power is the goal of the managerial elite. Why? It is simply that the complexity, speed, size, and range of changes within management today are all so fundamental and drastic that influence skills are at a premium.

The changing macroenvironment

Six interrelated forces within the macroenvironment have created this management revolution. These are: (1) technology, (2) economic factors, (3) finance, (4) the internationalization and globalization of business, (5) political forces, and (6) social forces.

■ Technology

Technological progress and the accompanying avalanche of open-access information have significantly altered the traditional power base of managers. Before the advent of computers, managers derived power and influence from the information and knowledge which they held. Departments and job roles were closely ring-fenced, meaning that all incoming and outgoing information had to pass by the "gates" manned by the respective manager. This "gatekeeper" role gave power to the manager, both inside his own domain and over outsiders.[10]

> Technological progress and the avalanche of open-access information have significantly altered the traditional power base of managers.

The computers which previously held information for access only via expert, gatekeeper managers, now allow anyone who needs information to get it themselves on-line without recourse to their managerial peers. As the *Wall Street Journal* put it:

"Computer-shy executives probably won't make it to the top of the company of 2000. Not that computer wizards or techies will be taking over – far from it. 'The computer in the basement is a utility, not a source of competitive advantage,' says Gerald R. Faulhaber, an associate professor at Wharton. Rather, chief executives will have to be comfortable exchanging information electronically and dealing with the ensuing organizational changes ... (William McGowan, the chief executive of MCI Communications Corp.) estimates that 15 percent of chief executives now get their information electronically. By 2000, he predicts, 'you'll have a hard time finding one who isn't computer-linked to the rest of his firm.'"[11]

Managers who previously sought and held power purely by hoarding and dispensing data now have less control. The scale and speed of these changes are dramatic – it is estimated that by the year 2000, the world Information Technology industry will be worth $600 billion and overtake oil as the world's largest industry.[12] National boundaries are no barrier to communication – telecommunication companies such as the UK company Cable and Wireless are competing aggressively to provide a range of international and global management information services.

This change is affecting every managerial profession. Today's trainee doctors can call upon expert diagnostic systems at the touch of a button. Accountants are deskilled with the introduction of computer-aided accounting systems. Computers in City of London dealing rooms now work automatically long after the human dealers have gone home in order to provide a 24-hour analysis of market potential or threat.

It is not technology alone, however, which has altered the traditional power base of managers. Rather, it is technology combined with its impact on organizational structure. Like corporate weight-watchers, businesses are hurriedly shedding layers and becoming flatter. Whole layers of middle management previously involved in coordination and control positions have been cut out – it has not been unusual for companies to go from seven, eight, or even nine levels of management down to as few as four or five. Although management theorists such as Harold Leavitt and Thomas Whisler predicted some 30 years ago that computerization would "lean" middle management, few foresaw the true severity of downsizing.[13] Industry insiders suggest that nearly

600,000 middle- and upper-level executives lost their jobs in the USA between 1984 and 1986.[14] Blue-chip companies such as GE, Ford, IBM, Shell, and BP have all participated in the process, leading *Business Week* to dub the managers "sitting ducks."[15]

The world authority on corporations, Rosabeth Moss Kanter, argues that flat organizations in which information is freely available require people to work in horizontal teams, rather than by invoking the power of a vertical hierarchy.[16] To use her celebrated phrase, the "crutch of unchallengeable authority" previously provided by a manager's position has been thrown away – in its place comes the need to "juggle constituencies, rather than control subordinates."[17] This juggling act involves all the softer skills of forming partnerships, seeking cooperation, and achieving consensus, rather than resorting to control mechanisms and unilateral decisions. In the words of a manager at Digital:

> "There is a big difference from a boss–subordinate relationship where the boss tells the subordinate, 'Here is the task at hand and please complete it,' and one where the boss says, 'We have got to win and here is what winning is as we see it. Is this how you see it?' In this new relationship we say, 'Let's talk about the work that has got to get done and let's divide up the tasks in a fashion that makes sense.' There is a very different way that you are going to be motivated and approach your work with that second scenario."[18]

Skills such as gathering information, resisting preconceived ideas, listening to others, building a consensus, consulting, collaborating, negotiating, appreciating the needs of others, correctly interpreting culture and style, self-presentation and so on, are all aspects of the modern manager's ability successfully to exercise interpersonal and social influence. Information technology plus organizational change have combined, therefore, to make influence skills come of age.

■ Economic factors

Perhaps the only economic factor which can be predicted with any certainty nowadays is unpredictability. In contrast, the 1950s and 1960s demonstrated a relatively consistent economic cycle.

As Bennett Harrison and Barry Bluestone argue in their classic text, *The Great U-Turn*,[19] inferior foreign competition, sluggish internal competition, a reputation for product innovation, and best management practice all lulled American and European companies into a false sense of security. This was the heyday of the towering bureaucracies which imposed order and direction down from on high.

Heightened international competition was one of the key factors which killed the complacency in the mid-1960s: however, it had a dramatic impact on corporate profitability. It was as if the towering bureaucracies had not seen it coming. Domestic markets developed into global markets, where products from Europe and America competed savagely with products of equal or superior quality from the newly industrialized countries.

Added to this heightened international competition was the speed of change generated by new technology. In the world of computers, for example, the capacity of computer chips has doubled every 18 months on average since the early 1960s, in accordance with Moore's law.[20] The consequent impact on product obsolescence of such exponential improvement is nothing short of dramatic.

These types of fundamental driving forces meant that organizations had to be much more flexible and adaptable in order to survive by taking advantage of rapidly evolving economic, market, and product opportunities. To compete successfully, organizations literally had to change shape. Gone were the vertical bureaucracies of the past. In came the horizontal designs of the 1990s.

Chief executive officers began to realize that things were moving too fast for them to be personally in touch with changing competitor strategy and product innovation. Instead, they had to share responsibility with teams who could no longer hide behind bureaucratic structures, avoiding direct responsibility for projects and decisions. These teams had to be close to the customer and the marketplace, and able to exert influence right across the organization to achieve results at speed.[21]

As demonstrated in *A Passion for Excellence*,[22] top managers could no longer be effective by heroically trying to be responsible for everything. Instead, they had to make heroes out of their subordinates by empowering them to share responsibility. Those subordinates who now possessed this responsibility had to be able to exercise influence effectively to get their ideas and proposals across and to win approval for projects. Sharing responsibility and gaining full participation both put a premium on the ability to influence.

■ Finance

Rising competition, underpinned by rapid technological change, demanded high levels of finance to support an organization's ability to react with speed by introducing new products and by improving service levels.

One of the principal ways in which organizations began to maximize revenue and profit was to relocate businesses to those regions around the world which provided the most favorable conditions, whether low manufacturing cost, highly skilled labour, or tax incentives. As one IBM manager told a reporter, "IBM has to be concerned with the competitiveness and well-being of any country or region that is a major source of IBM revenue."[23]

The growing importance of world business creates a demand for managers skilled both at working with people from other countries, and at using influence via a whole host of networks and alliances transcending those countries. In this situation, influence replaces authority as the key device for bringing multiple sets of constituencies together.

■ The internationalization and globalization of business

The massive economic and social upheavals of the 1980s, together with recent technological advances, have accelerated the trend toward the growing internationalization of business. Without question, the world is becoming one market.

In Europe, for example, the old national champion companies which were created to nurture and protect key domestic businesses from the onslaught of US multinationals, are transforming themselves into global webs with no particular connection with their own countries.[24] For example, Fujitsu, Japan's largest computer company, has acquired Britain's ICL; similarly, BMW, having taken over Rover from British Aerospace, is now making engines for Rolls-Royce cars.[25]

What holds true for products is equally true for services – in the management consultancy sector, Coopers & Lybrand Europe was established to encourage pan-European networking across the company and to allow pan-European industry groups to be developed. The company recognized that clients increasingly required single-contact access to teams with a pan-European focus.

The new transnational economy, as described by Peter Drucker,[26] does more than create new competitive challenges; it also increases yet further the importance of effective influence skills. Why? Because the global manager's task is now to put things together worldwide. Robert Reich, writing in the *Harvard Business Review*, has identified a global classic: Mazda's MX-5 Miata sports car was designed in California, financed from Tokyo and New York, prototyped in Worthing (England) for eventual assembly in Michigan and Mexico from advanced electrical components designed in New Jersey and manufactured in Japan.[27]

Projects such as the MX-5 above highlight the growing demand for managers who are sophisticated in international management and skilled at working with people from other countries. It is difficult for authoritarian individuals who rely on command and control strategies to work with people from other countries – successfully bringing together diverse, heterogeneous groups requires the full gamut of influence skills.

The structures which drive these global organizations are based around cosmopolitan management teams. Robert Reich reports that IBM, for example, prides itself on having five different nationalities represented among its highest ranking officers and three different nationalities among its external directors.[28] Four nationalities are represented on Unilever's Board, three on that of Shell Oil.

The ability to work with these cosmopolitan teams is complicated by the changed nature of these teams. Instead of an autocratic chief executive, the top of these organizations is run much more on a consensus-based model rather than on the command-style of management.

The Wall Street Journal has eloquently compared its vision of the global chief executive in the year 2000 with his predecessor:

"Since World War II, the typical corporate chief executive officer has looked something like this:

"He started out as a finance man with an undergraduate degree in accounting. He methodically worked his way up through the company from the controller's office in a division, to running that division, to the top job. His military background shows: He is used to giving orders – and to having them obeyed. As the head of the United Way drive, he is a big man in his community. However, the first time he traveled overseas on business was as chief executive. Computers make him nervous.

"But peer into the executive suite of the year 2000 and see a completely different person.

"His undergraduate degree is in French literature, but he also has a joint MBA/engineering degree. He started in research and was quickly picked out as a potential CEO. He zigzagged from research to marketing to finance. He proved himself in Brazil by turning around a failing joint venture. He speaks Portuguese and French and is on a first-name basis with commerce ministers in half a dozen countries. Unlike his predecessor's predecessor, he isn't a drill sergeant. He is first among equals in a five-person Office of the Chief Executive."[29]

Such global chief executives will achieve consensus through persuasion and negotiation, together with all of the softer skills which represent the components of influencing others. Whereas in the 1960s, only 8 percent of American companies had a team of three to six top officers led by the chairman, that figure had risen to 25 percent by 1984.[30]

Jack Sparks, ex-chairman of Whirlpool, is another who suggests that undergraduate studies should focus on the softer skills to allow future chief executives to work with and through people in the new global business arena.[31]

■ Political forces

This massive economic upheaval was accompanied by a profound shift in the attitude of governments, both in the UK and in the USA, toward deregulation of business, privatization plus encouragement of social and professional mobility.

UK examples of the process include privatization of the national utilities, British Telecom and British Railways; deregulation of financial services; and the encouragement of personal (portable) pensions to encourage social mobility.

Outside the USA and UK, many of the political barriers protecting organizations against competition were swept away in the 1980s and 1990s. At the start of the 1990s, for example, the command economies of eastern Europe and the former Soviet Union were dismantled, and the then European Community (EC) agreed with the European Free Trade Association (EFTA) to establish a European Economic Area (EEA). With a combined population of some 300 million across 19 countries, the EEA's free trade zone covered 43 percent of world trade. The list goes on, with countries such as India, South Korea, Brazil, and China all relaxing barriers and opening up to world competition.

These combined factors meant that all organizations felt the forces for change, and companies like IBM began to be exposed to competition on a worldwide scale. The deregulation of financial institutions, the opening up of the professions such as accountancy, law, medicine, and engineering are all driving the same dramatic changes in organizational structure and in the role of the employee.

Professionals now have to learn how to influence their customers and their competitors because no longer are they protected by the previous client–expert relationship. In the UK, for example, the civil service is being asked to compete and bid in an open market to perform its traditionally sacrosanct functions. It now has to learn to persuade a whole range of decision makers, as well as the public, that it provides value for money. The Home Office is currently contemplating putting out to tender activities as diverse as the Criminal Injuries Compensation Board and customs control at ports, while the health minister has recently put the Health Education Council out to tender. Indeed, certain National Health Service trusts are apparently now battling with their doctors to put the business needs of the organization before the needs of the patients.

■ Social forces

Another factor pushing organizations toward the greater use of influence rather than authority is the changing character of the workforce.

Educated modern employees now have modern expectations about work. In the old days, employees who had never gone to college were grateful to have steady work and a gradually rising standard of living. Consequently, most were relatively compliant and willing to accept direction.

Multilayered bureaucracies made jobs simple and as clearly defined as possible so that ordinary people could successfully perform them, while leaving the boss to make all the decisions. In 1996, an estimated 12 percent of UK employees are educated to degree level.[32] Consequently, they bring with them expectations which are entirely different from those of their predecessors: they want to be consulted; they do have ideas; they want to take on responsibility and use their initiative.

> In 1996, an estimated 12 percent of UK employees are educated to degree level. Consequently, they bring with them expectations which are entirely different from those of their predecessors.

This degree-educated class is not interested in safe, dull careers, doing boring routine tasks under the direction and control of someone else. Instead, they want to take shortcuts to get to the top of the corporate ladder. They are hungry to embrace the challenges of flatter, leaner organizations. They actively welcome the chance to use their influence skills to bypass the traditional authority-based routes to the top.

The implications for organizations

How did businesses respond to the new competitive pressure? The vast majority of businesses have undergone a revolution and literally changed shape. The impact of this revolution has been experienced in organizational structures as well as in the nature of managerial work.

■ New organizational structures

Corporations have radically restructured their internal hierarchies, "vertically disintegrating" their large, highly centralized industrial organizations. They have become much flatter in structure, having cut out many of the middle managers who previously occupied coordination and control roles.

British Steel is said to have once had an organization chart which unfolded to the width of an entire room.[33] Such vast pyramidal charts tend no longer to exist. *Fortune* magazine highlighted Jack Welch at GE for having "collapsed GE's management structure, a wedding cake that had towered up to nine layers high, and scraped off its ornate frosting of corporate staff."[34]

Rosabeth Moss Kanter has identified many striking examples of rampant restructuring:

> "Interested in cutting costs as well as improving delegation downward, a telephone company – once among the most intricately graded of organizations – has almost eliminated an entire managerial level ... and has doubled supervisory spans of control in its largest unit, which covers 75 percent of all employees.
>
> "An auto giant took its first step toward streamlining by banning all one-to-one reporting relationships (a boss responsible for only one subordinate).
>
> "A widely respected household products manufacturer has gradually thinned its line management ranks by creating 'high-commitment work systems' in which employee teams take full responsibility for production, without requiring managers.
>
> "A pharmaceutical company is 'delayering' ... to reduce unnecessary levels that were indeed 'delayers' of decisions and actions; it has distributed to all departments a kit of instructions for rearranging the organization chart to work without at least two levels of management.
>
> "An oil company, calling itself an 'elephant learning to dance,' is trying to become more agile by collapsing several levels of the management hierarchy."[35]

Nowadays, organizations will typically have three or four levels at most, with small units of teams, project groups or partners forming the organization's building blocks, rather than individuals in specialist or functional, hierarchical positions. Smaller units are faster, more focussed, more flexible, more friendly, and more fun – to borrow Kanter's five Fs.[36] Richard Branson, for example, favors units of 50 or 60, coordinated by a small centre of just five. These project teams themselves may be either permanent or temporary.

The notion of a permanent, life-long management career in one single organization has disappeared. Managers are increasingly brought into the organization on short-term contracts to work on particular projects or product events. In the 1970s, Alvin Toffler[37] coined the term "ad-hocracy" in *Future Shock* to describe his vision of a future world of free-form, constantly varying organizational structures.

Organizations have not only changed internal structure, but also their internal *modus operandi*. This applies equally to ongoing internal services which may be outsourced – National Health Hospitals in Britain, for example, have contracted out catering facilities to specialist catering companies – as it does to one-off needs. Instead of organizations operating independently, with a plethora of internal departments covering all aspects of business activity, organizations now tend to link or hook up with other organizations for specific projects, products, or services. Such contracted-out services include payroll management, logistics, invoicing, database management, product design, legal services, and personnel management. There are economies to be gained from such operations – an organization accesses particular expertise only when it is needed, rather than carrying the fixed overhead of maintaining that expertise in-house.

Raymond Miles describes these new, emerging organizational forms as "the dynamic network model," in which the key role is that of the broker, who puts it all together.[38] We can think of Bob Geldof as fulfilling an archetypal broker role when he organized the epoch-making *Band Aid* project, uniting for a common cause artists, broadcasters, politicians, revenue collectors, and charity workers alike through his influence.

> Nowadays, organizations will typically have three or four levels at most, with small units of teams, project groups or partners forming the organization's building blocks, rather than individuals in specialist or functional, hierarchical positions.

The 1991 British Institute of Management Survey *The Flat Organization: Philosophy and Practice*[39] revealed the following facts:

- Almost nine out of ten of the participating organizations are in the process of becoming slimmer and flatter.
- In some eight out of ten of the participants, more work is being done in teams and a more responsive network organization is being created.
- Over two thirds of the participants acknowledge that functions are becoming more interdependent and that procedures and permanence are giving way to flexibility and temporary arrangements.
- Over two thirds of respondents thought that organizations should become more interdependent.

RECENT
FINDINGS

■ The new manager

Flatter delayered organizations have caused management to shrink as a separate organizational class, with responsibility for planning, coordinating, and controlling the output of others.

Shrinking middle management means that those who are left in management have an increased span of responsibility, and are perhaps controlling projects for which they have little technical expertise or understanding.

DEFINITION

In this scenario, achievement of results using a one-man model of leadership and tight control, with total responsibility vested in the leader, will not work. The manager will not only find it physically impossible to spend the amount of time necessary for checking-up, keeping-up, and sweeping-up, he will also lack the expertise to absorb the technical information effectively and competently, or on a more basic level, even the ability to access it.

Achievement of outstanding results through large, flat groupings of teams is only possible when all employees and partners feel a sense of shared responsibility for success. And this is only possible when you sweep aside the crutch of formal authority and control, and aim for mutual gain and success through a model of participation and interdependence. Participation and interdependence require people to influence and to be influenced. This influence is required at all points of contact: from the boss to the team; from the team to the boss; within the team; across multiple, linked-up teams and so on.

Executives at all levels will need to know how to sell important projects, persuade colleagues to provide needed resources, create satisfactory working relationships with people, insist that the bosses respond to issues that may not be important to them, and in turn give thoughtful responses to the requests which their associates make of them. Competition is out; cooperation through influence is in.

The management of employees in the contract and flexible sectors will also require the same skills of relationship building and influence.

You could argue that in these sectors, the core can exercise sufficient control by holding the purse strings in order to ensure delivery of results, but this is an oversimplification. Anyone who has ever hired domestic help, whether an electrician, builder, cleaner, or childminder – knows the difference between getting the job done according to the minimum specification and to a quality level which encourages you to use the same service again. A quality job is usually achieved where both parties have managed to successfully influence each other to develop a shared understanding through clear communication and by so doing, achieve agreement on objectives, methods, and results.

Many of the bonds and loyalties which encourage people to go the extra mile cannot be specified in written contracts through endless subclauses. Instead, they are built and developed through successful interpersonal influence.

It will be up to managers in the core to influence all the parties with whom they work. To achieve the best quality and added-value results for their businesses, they must be fully aware of, and competent in, influencing strategies. With so much interdependence required, the wielding of influence becomes the real test of skill for the manager of the 1990s.

CHAPTER SUMMARY

- This chapter has examined the relationship between managerial effectiveness and influence skills.

- It has assessed the changing nature of organizations in the 1990s, and the technological, economic, financial, political, social, and global forces which are driving that change.

- It has identified the nature of the new flatter organizational structures with fewer managers, but with networks of interlocking project teams, which may spin across a number of linked organizations.

- We have seen the emergence of a new managerial role which moves away from control and authority toward interdependence and participation. With so much interdependence, the skill to influence effectively was identified as the real test of management competence in the 1990s.

CONCEPT QUIZ

Do you understand the basic need for influence skills in organizations in the 1990s?

Answer each question either "True" or "False". Compare your answers with those at the foot of the page.

Remember to go back and check your understanding of any question which you get wrong.

1. Management is primarily concerned with planning, organizing, and controlling. *True or false?*

2. Position in the hierarchy is the key tool through which managers get things done in the 1990s. *True or false?*

3. Managers are judged by what they do rather than who they know and get on with. *True or false?*

4. Most management decisions are made on logical, rational criteria. *True or false?*

5. The development of influence skills is as important as technical competence in today's flatter organizations. *True or false?*

6. Flat, delayered network-based organizations require a consensus style, not a control style of management. *True or false?*

7. Intelligent knowledge workers automatically respect management authority and discipline. *True or false?*

8. Financial control alone ensures a first-class job in the contract and peripheral sectors. *True or false?*

9. It is best management practice to focus on the task and forget the people. *True or false?*

10. The ability to work through interpersonal influence becomes even more vital in modern, transnational, global organizations. *True or false?*

Answers

1(F), 2(F), 3(F), 4(F), 5(T), 6(T), 7(F), 8(F), 9(F), 10(T).

THE CEREBRAL MANAGER

Laura Jones had just been promoted to the post of marketing director in a large manufacturing company, an autonomous subsidiary of its US parent organization. She was very excited about her new position and proudly told her husband, Neil, that with her new title and position of authority, she had at last achieved the power to put into practice all the ideas and knowledge she had developed when she did her MBA.

She believed that she would also have the full backing of the managing director, James, who had given her the impression during the interview process that he was a rational, results-driven person like herself. Laura was also sure that James's naval background meant respect for hard work and analysis.

During the first months in the job, Laura focussed on a strategic analysis of the market, the health of the product portfolio, and on the implementation of basic marketing information systems.

James gave Laura a glowing appraisal after six months. At the end of the appraisal interview, James asked Laura where she saw her career developing over the next five years. Laura answered that she would like James's job as MD, believing that this truthful answer would not make James feel threatened. After all, James was now approaching 60 and she saw him as a father figure who would happily assume the role of her mentor and groom her for greater things.

Somewhat naively, Laura did not review her first impression of James when she heard stories about him from one of her brand managers. Not only was James a sailing fanatic, he was also a confirmed partygoer with a reputation for ensuring that he had a good time.

The second half of the year proved rather turbulent for Laura. Her analysis of the market revealed that although the company's overall product portfolio was still profitable, the latest product launch initiated under the auspices of James had not done as well as expected. Far from being a rising star, the latest product was already a falling star, losing market share as well as money. Laura presented this information to James, who seemed somewhat reluctant to take it on board. She was puzzled by James's reaction, but kept up her hard work planning a relaunch of the ailing product.

At the weekly team meetings, Laura started to feel that James was happier indulging in sea stories than in detailed discussion of the market and product performance. At any mention of information technology, James's eyes would glaze over – it was as if computers made him nervous.

At the expense of her family life, however, Laura continued her 70-hour weeks and achieved a significant increase in market share for the relaunched product within the first 18 months.

At her next appraisal, Laura duly expected a glowing report. She was all the more shocked, therefore, to find James highly critical of her performance and unwilling to acknowledge the increase in market share and profits. The more that Laura attempted to argue her case, the more critical James became in his assessment. Laura told her husband, Neil, that evening and they both wondered what had gone wrong.

Review questions

1. Why did Laura's new job go so badly wrong?

2. What could Laura have done differently?

3. What does the case illustrate about the need for influence skills?

SUMMARY CHECKLIST

❑ Focus on the people as well as the task.

❑ Avoid using just logic and fact.

❑ Be aware of the network of people with whom you need to make contact.

❑ Be aware of the hidden agendas of colleagues.

❑ Be aware of the need to manage emotional and irrational reactions.

❑ Be aware that people do not all share the same goals.

❑ Work through achieving consensus rather than control.

❑ Get to know your network of colleagues off the job as soon as possible.

❑ Build personal relationships with colleagues at the beginning of the job.

ACTION CHECKLIST

1. Identify the major technological, economic, and financial changes which have had an impact on your organization.

   _____

   _____

2. How have these changes affected the way your organization is structured? Has your company delayered?

   _____

   _____

3. How has your job changed? Do you spend more time working in teams without direct authority over the other team members, for example?

   _____

   _____

4. What positive attempts do you make to build a good working relationship with colleagues?

_____

_____

5. Do you start building a good relationship from the earliest possible moment?

_____

_____

6. List the various reasons why you would like to improve your level of influence skills.

_____

_____

7. Identify those people you have been most successful in influencing. Do these people share common characteristics? What does this tell you about your strengths and weaknesses in successfully influencing others?

_____

_____

8. Do you use different types of strategies and tactics with different types of worker, and also across different countries?

_____

_____

9. Describe how you feel when someone ignores your contribution on a successful project?

_____

_____

10. Describe how you feel when all team members successfully agree on how to reach a mutually agreed objective.

_____

_____

WHAT DOES IT MEAN TO USE INFLUENCE?

This chapter focuses on understanding the process of exercising influence. It examines the concept and nature of influence and its relationship with power. It looks at the *seven power levers* open to the manager in organizations in the 1990s. It examines the *six principles of influence* which can unleash latent power.

SELF–ASSESSMENT EXERCISE

A power/influence analysis of your position

A good way to begin understanding how power and influence may be preventing you from getting things done is to list the people and positions upon which you depend. The example presented below focuses on a managing director.

Figure 1
Analyzing the power/influence of your position

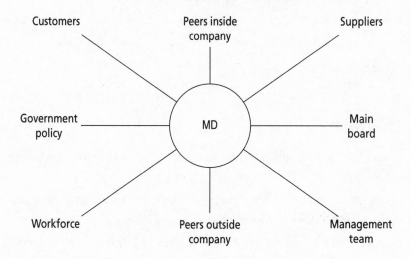

When you have completed your own version of **Figure 1, answer** the following questions:

1. Describe the basis of dependence in each case: does it concern the party's position, resource power, information power, connections, expertise, the sanctions which that party may be able to use against you, or the position of authority held by that party?

   _____

   _____

2. How important is each case of dependence?

   _____

   _____

3. What strategies and tactics do you use to try and change the balance of power in each case of dependence? For example, do you ever:

(a) consider the context and style in which you present proposals?

(b) consider the timing and order in which you present things?

(c) withhold information or resources?

(d) build up a consensus among your colleagues to develop support for your proposal?

(e) ingratiate yourself with your influence targets?

(f) use inspirational or emotional appeals to create support and commitment?

(g) actively network and build relationships?

_____

_____

_____

_____

Follow-up

This activity was designed to help you analyze the power/influence base of your job.

It is probable that you feel that your ability to get things done is hindered by the lack of power associated with your position. However, you may well be overlooking the various sources of power available to you, falling into the trap of thinking that power is all related to position.

If you answered "No" to most of the statements in question three, then you are not using the strategies and tactics of influence which could effectively alter the various power bases in your job.

What the exercise should certainly demonstrate is that there is more to getting things done than the position you hold. In fact, not only are there many different types of power which we can access, there are also many different influence strategies and tactics which we can apply to activate those types of power. This chapter examines this relationship between power and influence.

Why power and influence?

The inability to get things done, to have ideas and decisions implemented, is widespread in organizations today. And as we have seen in chapter one, this problem seems to be getting worse. Many of the problems of implementation which managers experience are often connected with a manager's inability to influence effectively and to unleash the sources of power available to him or her.

Managers get things done in organizations through the process of power and influence. Individual effort, ability, and achievement are not enough. Organizational life is not a meritocracy which rationally allocates rewards, resources, and recognition to those who produce the best results. If it were, then many of those who are now reading this book would have no need to do so.

How many times have we all become frustrated when a colleague successfully wins approval for a proposal backed by only a superficial level of analysis, merely because he or she has successfully harnessed the principles of contrast, commitment, and scarcity in order to key into the mind set of the organization and boss?

Think of the power you can have by being part of the "club" in the organization. Consider how influential that could be for fast–track promotion. Don't forget the power of liking and of being liked – and the allowances which are then made for the right kind of person. And don't underestimate the potency of emotion, the benefits of concealing your own feelings and ambitions, the rewards from playing the nonthreatening backroom boy until the time for your succession is right.

The fact that these influence skills can be manipulative and covert does not rob them of legitimacy. They are an intrinsic and important part of behavior in every organization, and each is based on valid psychological principles. And even if you consider not using the techniques yourself, do remember that all those around you certainly are using them, probably at your expense. So let's consider the relationship between power and influence.

What is power?

In our terms, power is the potential ability to influence and get things done in organizations. It is a latent resource which must be unleashed by other processes.

This unleashing of the manager's power relies on the process of influence. In turn, influence as a process relies on interpersonal and social pressure to spur other people to change their attitudes, behavior, and decisions to comply with your requests.

What potential power sources are open to the would–be influencer?

The seven power levers

Academic commentators can discuss at great length the myriad sources of power open to individuals in organizations. We will focus on the seven key sources into which the potential influencer can tap. These can be summarized as: (1) resource power, (2) information, (3) expertise, (4) connections, (5) coercion, (6) position, and (7) personal power.

The first six sources of power are organizationally based, whilst the seventh source – personal power – derives from the way you behave as an individual.

■ Resource power

If you have control over various kinds of resources, then you will be perceived as powerful. Resources can be anything that is perceived to be valuable – from the control of budgets, major investments, hiring and firing, remuneration, and staff promotions, right down to the allocation of parking spaces in the company parking lot.

A leading Harvard academic, Jeffrey Pfeffer, has identified two of the most important resources for any member of the flat organization of the 1990s: allies and supporters.[1] Organizations are increasingly interdependent systems in which it is difficult to get things done by yourself.

It is vital to have loyal, trusted supporters to help carry out your plans. Witness the failure of Hillary Clinton to get her 1994 health care plan accepted, in large part because she failed to develop a significant base of support in the American Congress.

Resources can be nonmaterial (e.g. status) just as easily as material (e.g. money). Playing the master magician and conjuring nonmaterial resources out of a tophat is particularly effective. For example, if you know that a subordinate whom you wish to influence is susceptible to status and privilege, then giving him a masterkey to the building, making a corporate credit card available to him, or allowing him to sit in on a meeting with higher management, all become potential tactics.

> Pfeffer has identified two of the most important resources for any member of the flat organization of the 1990s: allies and supporters.

Withholding from your target direct access to key people or facilities is an equally effective use of nonmaterial resources – it could be as simple as withdrawing the master key from a previous keyholder, or reducing the level of capital spending an executive may incur without obtaining prior authorization.

President Lyndon Johnson exemplified the principle of creating power by withholding direct access to key people when he was a student at Southwestern Texas State Teachers College.[2] His actual job as special assistant to the college president's personal secretary was restricted to passing messages from the president to the rest of the faculty. Johnson skillfully enlarged the job so that messages were sent back via him as well. Occupying a desk in the president's outer office, he also took it upon himself to announce visitors, and gradually escalated his role into that of a full–blown appointments secretary. It was not long before Johnson was viewed as the exclusive gatekeeper to the college president.

What is important is understanding what people want – for example, access to individuals, status, or information – and then controlling and delivering the things which people want.

You should always be on the lookout for new resources which you could exploit, whether that is control over equipment, time, or budgets.

Having a resource in itself, however, does not make an individual powerful. Rather, it is the control over the resource which really counts, and by control we mean the ability to exercise complete discretion over its use. For example, the manager of a company's logistics department may delegate the timetabling for truck drivers to subordinates, but if they have to continually go to the manager for authorization, they remain powerless in the eyes of colleagues.

■ Information is power

The old saying that information is power certainly holds true in today's organizations. Information which offers potential power in organizations falls into three main groups.

Technical information

This is the information which comes from the facts contained in reports and records, whether financial or operational. They can all provide important insights into the management effectiveness of the organization.

Consider the example of Tiny Rowland, the merchant adventurer who founded the Lonrho trading empire, who was so enraged by the efforts of the Australian, Alan Bond, to buy Lonrho in 1989 that he got his financial accountant, Terry Robinson, to prepare and then publish such a damning 93–page financial report on Bond's business empire that the latter went out of business, and suffered a nervous breakdown into the bargain.

Who you are and what your role is normally define the type of information you can get hold of. However, you can increase your access to technical knowledge by carefully positioning yourself in the organization's communication and social infrastructure. By building relationships with powerful individuals in the organiza-

tion, or sometimes even with the processors of sensitive data –
secretaries and clerks, for example – you can create channels to
privileged information.

Information on the organization's social system

As with technical information, your knowledge of how people
feel about each other and the organization can be a potent source
of power. In addition, you can take positive steps to increase this
inside knowledge by building relationships and networking
across all levels of the organization. It could be as simple as cultivating a relationship with the personal assistant to the chairman,
for example, which would then give you access to the chairman's
thinking about people and policies.

Tony Berry, former Chairman of Blue Arrow Ltd, is a particularly good example of someone whose climb to the top was made
easier by a relationship which brought him close to an important
contact.[3] After ten years at Guinness, Berry was approached for a
job as chief accountant by the financial director of Bovril, whose
secretary just happened to be Berry's first wife. As Berry himself
put it: "It really was a bit of a set–up; as ever, it's not what you
know, it's who you know … I certainly wasn't qualified for the
job, for which they paid me an exorbitant salary."[4]

Personal information

You have only to think of British parliamentary whips and their
supposed use of the black book of compromising information to
control backbenchers to realize the power of personal information.

Voluntarily disclosing personal information is a two–edged
sword: it can contribute to the process of building trust in a relationship, but it also represents a weapon which can be turned
against you, should the relationship go bad. The British monarchy's apparent efforts to include a confidentiality clause in the

divorce settlement between the Prince and Princess of Wales clearly illustrate the point.

■ The power of expertise

This type of power is gained by having specialist knowledge or skill in a particular field. Financiers, computer specialists, and lawyers can all exploit expertise not available to others.

Nick Leeson, the so–called "rogue trader" of Barings Bank, so convincingly presented his expertise in the highly complex world of financial derivatives that his managers neglected to monitor his performance, and thus contributed to the loss of the bank's inde-pendence.

■ The power of connections

If you operate a wide network of influential personal and profes-sional contacts outside the organization as well as inside, then you can be said to have powerful connections.

As flamboyant entrepreneur Peter de Savary put it:

> "... I would not have done what I have done without many, many "guardian angels" or many helping hands along the way. ... A lot of people have helped me over a long period and I think you need that help to the end of your days."[5]

Lionel Green played a similar mentor role for Jennifer d'Abo, an extremely successful entrepreneur and chairman of Moyses Stevens Investments. As she put it:

> "I loved that man more than anyone else in the world; he invented me. He was a great entrepreneur in his own right. He was the kind-est, most generous giver. I met him when I was about 21. When I went into business he gave me my trade references. He had to make them up as we went along because I didn't have any. Whenever I needed advice, or whenever I was going to do something dotty, like buying a bankrupt department store, Lionel would say: 'Oh wonderful darling,

wonderful, what a good idea. Come over and talk to me about it.'
Then he would have a whole list of names of people to give me for
advice. He was a star."[6]

The professional application of social contacts is demonstrated by
the case of Lord Young, Conservative trade minister in the late
1980s, who was talent–spotted by Isaac Wolfson at a wedding at
which Lord Young delivered the best man's speech. Recognizing
Lord Young's communication skills, Wolfson appointed him to
Great Universal Stores.[7]

Contacts made in such a way may not always be immediately
productive, but they still have the ability to deliver results at a
later date. This means that simply making contacts with people
who could be useful in the future is worthwhile, whether by
developing friendships at seminars and conferences, or by
exchanging your business card at meetings.

Failure to cultivate good contacts is dangerous. W. Richard
Goodwin, president and CEO of the Johns-Manville Corporation, delivered record sales and profit growth between 1970 and
1975. However, his failure to develop working relationships with
the board – partly because he was a natural individualist, and
partly because he relied on his successful performance to do the
talking – meant that he was forced to resign in 1976.

> "We had here a fellow who had no experience working with a group
> of people who held ultimate responsibility for the company … he was
> used to working as an individual before he joined Johns-Manville …
> he had trouble working with a Board."[8]

■ Coercive power

Many managers shy away from doing unpleasant things or using
what academics call a punishment–centered approach.[9] They are
often reluctant to make decisions over issues such as redundancy,
or relocation, even though they have the authority to do so in
their role or position.

Yet, you can derive enormous power from taking unpleasant actions which you believe to be commercially correct, provided that you implement these actions in a consistent way which allows people to retain their self–respect and dignity. How you use such authority is all–important in determining whether other people view it as a justified use of authority or as a punishment.

Jack Welch eliminated 100,000 jobs at General Electric (GE) in the early 1980s, initially earning him the soubriquet "Neutron Jack" (after the bomb which kills people but leaves buildings standing).[10] But it was the flair with which he conducted the necessary bloodletting, combined with the subsequent growth in GE's stock market valuation from $12 billion (1980) to $65 billion (1991), that earned him universal respect and transformed him into one of the major corporate heroes of the 1990s.

Media tycoon Rupert Murdoch implemented a highly effective punishment–centered approach in his dealings with the abrasive editor of the *Sun* newspaper, Kelvin MacKenzie:

> To keep his total control, Murdoch ruled by silence. His strategy was to make every one of his editors feel that his phone call, from whichever part of the empire he was currently inhabiting, was the most important event of the day or the week …
>
> Murdoch kept MacKenzie on his toes by making his calls at all times of day and night. They always followed the same format. 'Hello, Kelvin, how's it going? What's your splash?' MacKenzie would explain. A long intimidating pause would follow before there was a comment from the other end. If MacKenzie had done something 'naughty', he would sit worrying, waiting to see if he was to be bollocked or whether the matter would be ignored. Afterwards he would emerge, sighing with relief and saying: 'Thank Christ! He didn't mention it' …
>
> But sometimes it would be the most terrifying statement of all: 'You're losing your touch, Kelvin. [Pause] Your paper is pathetic. [Pause] You're losing your touch, Kelvin'. Then the phone would go down. After a call like this, life in the office would be hell for everyone."[11]

Some individuals are able to adopt a punishment–centered approach through the power of their individual physical attributes. Robert Maxwell, for instance, was apparently able to use his physical presence to induce others to comply.

■ The power of position

The most obvious source of power is your formal position, which allows you to get people to do what you want them to do. The ability to allocate tasks, establish priorities, arbitrate in decisions, set deadlines, and hire and fire people are all part of the manager's position power.

No one is omnipotent. You might imagine that a chief executive like Rupert Murdoch would have almost unlimited power associated with his position, but analysis would reveal that he is constrained by any number of variables in any given situation, such as the power of institutional investors or media–regulating governments.

Of course, the opportunities and constraints of any role are also heavily influenced by the support which the positionholder receives from other authority figures and by the resources supporting the positionholder.

Holding an apparently powerful position is not the same as holding power. An illustration of this was ex-Cabinet minister Norman Lamont's acerbic remark during late 1994 that prime minister "John Major was in power, but not in control."

Or take President Clinton, ostensibly the holder of the most prestigious and powerful position in the world, who is enormously constrained in his power to act because his party lost control of Congress in the 1994 midterm elections to the Republicans who subsequently blocked his access to vital resources.

As we saw in chapter one, the degree of power associated with position is diminishing with increased education levels and democratic values in society. People expect you to earn your authority through using your expertise. They also expect to be consulted and informed about what to do, rather than simply be told.

In addition, as organizations delayer and become progressively flatter, access to those positions which do represent a secure power base has inevitably become more constricted. In the brave new world of partners and coworkers, the crutch of formal authority has been kicked away.

■ Personal power

This type of power comes from making people feel attracted to you as a person.

Personality is a large part of the story here, but so too is physical presence and appearance. To a large extent, personality and physicality combine to produce "charisma," the ability not only to make people feel attracted to you, but also to then spur them on to do the things which you want.

> To successfully apply personal power, you must ensure that sufficient opportunities for interpersonal contact exist – it is difficult to project your charisma through the written word or the high-technology communications media which currently exist, such as video conferencing.

The personal power of British Labour Party leader Tony Blair is often favorably compared against that of the "grey" John Major. Similarly, Richard Branson has created a great deal of personal power through his youthful and energetic sporting endeavors which have attracted extremely high media coverage. TV pictures of President Clinton jogging create a positive impression when contrasted with the infamous TV image of President Carter collapsing out of exhaustion during a run.

Physical presence also confers a halo or horns effect – President Nixon was always said to have come across as devious on TV because of his heavy five o'clock shadow.

To successfully apply personal power, you must ensure that sufficient opportunities for interpersonal contact exist – it is difficult to project your charisma through the written word or the many high–technology communications media which currently exist, such as video conferencing.

What is influence?

Given that there are many different sources of power in organizations, why do managers still feel relatively powerless? To understand this, we should revisit our original definition of power which stated that power is the *potential* ability to influence. What this definition implies is that power is a latent resource which must be unleashed by other processes.

The key unleashing process is influence, which uses interpersonal and social skills to make others voluntarily change their attitudes to events, people, and decisions to enable your ideas to be implemented. In other words, managers can become truly powerful only when they develop the key skills involved in the process of influencing others.

That is not to say that you cannot use the various forms of power as resources in themselves to gain commitment to decisions and to change people's behavior. For example, you may be successful in gaining cooperation from a colleague by virtue of your superior position in the hierarchy, or by the power of your expertise over them on a particular project, or perhaps even through the power of your personality. But all these power strategies imply a degree of coercion. This may produce superficial behavioral changes, but not real, underlying changes in an individual's feelings or beliefs about a particular situation.

> Power is a latent resource which must be unleashed by other processes. The key unleashing process is influence, which uses interpersonal and social skills to make others voluntarily change their attitudes.

In strong contrast, influence is not coercive. It is a more subtle process which aims to change behavior, attitudes, and beliefs in a much more unconscious fashion. Yes, it certainly taps into those power resources, but it works through a subtle process of interpersonal and social persuasion. Influence is a much less visible process than naked power – by its very nature, it is indirect and subtle. Other people will not even be aware that you are using it. And this invisible and subtle nature instills influence with an internal force of its own.

Recall the example of Laura in chapter one. Although Laura had both position and expert power, she failed not only to impress her boss James with her powerful marketing analysis, but also to win recognition and approval for the subsequent increase in market share. She simply did not push the right buttons to key into James on an interpersonal and social level. Doing a good job was not enough – Laura did not influence James effectively.

> Influence is a much less visible process than naked power – by its very nature, it is indirect and subtle. Other people will not even be aware that you are using it.

■ Influence without power

Can executives and managers in organizations be influential without power? The plain truth is "No." Power is part of every organization, be it a large global corporation, a small manufacturing operation, a school, or local church. Even the humblest of us in an organization can exert some power – we can all *prevent* something even if we cannot *create* anything. Recall to mind the scene of the bus driver waiting for a passenger who is staggering forward, weighed down by baggage when, just before the passenger can reach the bus, the driver says: "Sorry, can't wait any longer."

Organizations are made up of interdependent people where differences and conflicts arise as part of normal everyday life. There are different degrees of commitment to the stated goals of the organization, probably even different levels of understanding of what these goals may be. All of these differences require reconciliation through the process of power and influence.

Most decision making in organizations reflects these myriad social and interpersonal factors. As a result, a technically skilled manager unaware of these factors is condemned to the life of an organizational hermit, with limited influence to accomplish anything.

As we have seen, there are so many different sources of power in organizations that everyone has the potential to access power in some form. Sometimes this access to power will be determined by the organization as part of a job role. At other times, power comes from an individual's personality and presence. In addition, the degree to which others are dependent on resources under your control has an impact on your potential power. To become truly influential, you must become aware of the different sources of power open to you and activate them effectively to get things done.

Many executives in organizations may think that they are powerless, but influential. This is a delusion. If they are influential, they must have power, whether that means having the ear of the boss, or even being granted special privileges in return for favors. Ultimately someone is conferring information or personal power upon them to make them influential.

Power and influence are inextricably linked. To be influential, you need to be able to exploit whatever power resources you have available to you. Certainly there are degrees of power and influence. For example, one person may have a fairly limited power base but be enormously influential (e.g. ex-Cabinet minister Willie Whitelaw, Mrs Thatcher's advisor), while another person may boast of enormous power resources, while he lacks the influence to take people with him (e.g. Michael Heseltine, current deputy prime minister of the Conservative Government, who failed to force through privatization of the Royal Mail in 1994).

■ Power without influence

Can you be powerful without being influential? Yes, there certainly are individuals who are powerful without necessarily being influential. Person A may get Person B to do something against B's wishes. Under such circumstances, the power levers are applied to achieve an immediate objective to the satisfaction of only one of the parties involved. On this basis, power is a fairly crude, unsophisticated manipulative approach to goal achievement – there is anecdotal evidence to suggest that Robert Maxwell abused power in this way. Because of its very crudity, however, it can only be used in certain situations, organizational cultures, and for certain intentions.

A more sophisticated use of power involves the skills of exercising influence.

The six principles of influence

How do we begin to create the strategies and tactics through which we begin to influence others? To understand how to do this, we must briefly turn to the principles of social psychology to help us better understand the basis of social interaction and why people agree and comply with our requests.

Social psychology tells us that six interrelated principles determine the success of every managerial attempt to use influence. Summarized these are: (1) contrast, (2) historical commitments and consistency, (3) scarcity value, (4) social proof, (5) liking and ingratiation, and (6) emotion. Three of the principles (contrast, historical commitments, and scarcity value) relate to how we "frame" or see things.[12] Accordingly, these principles stress the importance of understanding the context in which your proposals are presented. The remaining three principles (social proof, liking and ingratiation, and emotion) relate to how the actions of others influence us. These principles highlight the importance of managing your own actions, and those of others, on an interpersonal level.

■ Principle one: contrast

We see and experience the present in terms of the past. Dubbed by social psychologist Robert Cialdini[13] as the contrast effect, this provides us with a ready–made tool to evaluate the present proposal, event or person. During a selection interview, for example, the way in which we evaluate candidate B's performance will be significantly determined by the performance of the previous candidate, A. If candidate A performed badly, then a mediocre performance from candidate B would by contrast be rated more highly than it was in reality.

As Cialdini succinctly puts it, "if the second event is fairly different from the first, we will tend to see it as even more different then it actually is."[14] Cialdini describes how the contrast principle is often used to good effect in sales situations. If a person comes into a clothing shop to buy a suit and a sweater, the experienced salesman will sell the suit first. Having purchased the more expensive item, the customer will then see the sweater – even an expensive sweater – as being comparatively inexpensive. Conversely, if the less expensive item is presented first, the contrast principle suggests that the more expensive item will seem even more costly by comparison.

Real estate agents will use "set–up" properties, properties that are both undesirable and offered at inflated prices. After seeing such a property, the prospective buyer is much more likely to react favorably to a nicer, but still high–priced house because, by comparison, it seems like a bargain.[15]

The implications of the contrast principle for influencing our colleagues at work are clear. When we present a proposal, we should always carefully consider how favorably or unfavorably it will compare in the mind of the target with his or her previous experiences.[16] Agenda setting is, therefore, very important.

> If a person comes into a shop to buy a suit and a sweater, the experienced salesman will sell the (more expensive) suit first.

So it is always important to develop an understanding of your potential target's previous experiences, against which he or she will inevitably compare your proposal or action.

■ Principle two: historical commitments and consistency

Cialdini argues that we have an overwhelming desire to act consistently with previous commitments we have made to decisions and to people. Personal and interpersonal pressures make us behave in ways which justify these earlier decisions.[17]

He cites the telling example of the racetrack – after placing a bet, gamblers tend to be much more confident of their horse's chances of winning than they were immediately before laying down the bet. Nothing about the horse's chances of winning actually changes, of course; it is the same horse on the same track with the same jockey. But in the minds of those gamblers, its prospects improve significantly once that ticket is purchased.[18]

Withdrawing from previous commitments requires us to acknowledge that our previous thinking was flawed and that we must painfully reevaluate our decision.

Also, people who vacillate publicly are viewed as indecisive, whereas incisive consistency is valued as a true leadership trait.[19] It is said that the late Sir Keith Joseph never became leader of the British Conservative Party precisely because his high intellect allowed him to see both sides of an argument – so he appeared indecisive. In contrast, his protégée, Mrs Thatcher, was perhaps less intellectually brilliant, but became prime minister because she was able to come down consistently on one side of the argument. Not for nothing did her conference speechwriter steal the phrase, "The lady's not for turning!"

According to Gerald Salincik, the psychological evidence suggests that we become heavily bound by previous commitments when the choice was voluntary and free of external pressure; when the public visibility of the commitments precludes any denial of responsibility; when it is difficult to alter the commitments; and when our commitments have disclosed our true attitudes to others.[20]

In our case study in chapter one, we saw how Laura failed to gain recognition for her significant increase in market share, despite the problems of relaunching the lame duck product range initiated by James. Several reasons combined to prevent James from recognizing Laura's achievement. In the first place, he would have had to acknowledge a possible flaw in his initial decision to launch the new product range. In addition, the launch decision had not only been visible and public; it had also been made without external pressure. Furthermore, James could not easily rid himself of the problem by withdrawing the range from the market. And finally, any admission that his decision making was flawed would have led others (and himself) to question his attitudes, values, and subsequent business behavior.

Pfeffer identifies a number of key implications of the commitment principle for influencing others at work. One implication is that the best way to achieve anything is to arrange for the "target" to perform a specific action, however apparently trivial. Provided that the action is done voluntarily, it will necessarily commit the target.[21] This is the reason why car dealers encourage you to test drive a car, for example, and why manufacturers loan machinery on a trial basis.

Another key implication is that once the process of commitment has started, it is difficult to stop – the commitment becomes even more intense as time goes by. For example, Margaret Thatcher's commitment to the poll tax (the national scheme to radically overhaul local taxes) was so absolute that she persisted with it, despite the advice from her closest circle to ditch it and to lay the blame at another minister's door. She even publicly declared the tax as her own personal project. Accordingly, it was the dire unpopularity of the tax which directly caused her fall from power.

A further implication is that you can develop alliances by getting others to do favors for you. Once people have become committed to you or to your project, they become locked into your success, and anxious to avoid any failure on your behalf.

> Provided the action is done voluntarily, it will commit the target. This is the reason why car dealers encourage you to test drive a car.

Fourthly, we can persuade people to change commitments, provided that we give them a face-saving way out which leaves their concept of self consistent and intact. Laura, for example, might have been more successful in her attempts to influence James had she been able to suggest that James was not fully responsible for his past decision to launch an

> We can persuade people to change commitments provided that we give them a face-saving way out.

inappropriate product range – to suggest perhaps that James had been driven by external pressures or had been given incorrect professional advice. She could have gone on to agree that these factors naturally would have led James to act as he did, but that the situation had now changed, making James free to act in a different way. What Laura should not have done was to ask – even if only implicitly – "How could James have done something so ill–judged?".

■ Principle three: scarcity value

Cialdini highlights that things seem more valuable to us when they are less available.[22] This so–called scarcity principle is a means of encouraging others to make shortcut judgments.[23] We can economize on the amount of information which others need to process before making decisions because they know that the things which are difficult to get are typically better than those that are easy to get.

In addition, people hate to lose the freedom of action or choice, a factor upon which the scarcity principle deliberately plays. Whenever this freedom is limited or threatened, people want the freedom significantly more than before – this is called the psychological theory of "reactance."[24]

Cialdini cites the simple example of the phone ringing when you are midway through an interesting face–to–face conversation.[25] You inevitably answer the unknown telephone caller, because the caller has a scarcity value which your face–to–face partner does not possess. You feel unable to ignore the telephone and risk missing for good the information which it might have brought.

Many other illustrations of the scarcity principle are found in the sales arena, where exclusive offers, limited bargains and special editions are all used to entice customers to buy. In the 1980s, for instance, the policy of confectionery manufacturer, Cadbury, was to withdraw its best selling "Cream Eggs" from the market for a certain period each year, to cultivate what it termed "the strawberry syndrome" – the company understood that something too freely available risked losing its appeal. Similarly, an executive who has been head hunted into a new company tends to conjure up a much more valuable image in the staff's mind than a recruit who has merely responded to a traditional advertisement along with many other candidates.

What are the implications of the scarcity principle for using influence at work? Pfeffer identifies two in particular.[26]

In the first place, whatever you propose or suggest should always appear to be scarce and be on the point of being snapped up by somebody else. To succeed in job hunting, for example, you are well–advised always to present an image of being in demand from other organizations which are pressing you for a quick decision.

Scarcity can also apply to pricing: as the economists have it, price is an indicator of quality. This means that the higher the price, the more precious and desirable your product will seem. Marketing theory suggests that you should always raise the price of products you are about to kill off – sales often increase in the product's last death rattle. A further example can be seen in the field of consultancy – if a consultant's daily fee is very low, the company seeking to retain a consultant may make the shortcut judgment that the consultant's quality standard is equally low.

■ Principle four: social proof

Cialdini contends that we often rely on the opinions and behavior of others to help us discover the correct opinions and behaviors to demonstrate in particular organizational situations. This is dubbed "social proof."[27]

Relying on others is especially important when things are ambiguous. When you join a new company, for example, you have no idea how to behave, what the culture is, how you are expected to do your job. A salesman might not know whether the sales culture is concerned with ruthless, nonrepeat business where corners will be cut with customers, or whether the culture is all to do with long–term customer relationships built on mutual trust. In such situations, we watch what others do and say, rather than rely on the formal job description.

This desire to fit in with the general consensus can blind us to what is actually happening and can override our own judgment. For example, how often do we hear friends praise the food in a particular restaurant, although in reality the cuisine is very poor, purely because the restaurant has received excellent reviews in a socially correct food guide? Similarly, a salesman who "knows the industry inside out" and is presented as a model of excellence throughout the company may, in fact, be consistently missing his sales targets.

Advertisements will often use socially acceptable celebrities to prove that their product is similarly acceptable, whether it is tennis hero André Agassi, promoting the Pepsi relaunch, or Formula One racing driver Nigel Mansell advertising tires. Cloakroom attendants will often leave money in a tray on the counter as proof of the acceptability of tipping them. Similarly, in London's shopping mecca of Oxford Street, card sharps use "plants" who win money from them to entice innocent and unwary passers–by to join in as well.

In business, a positive consensus will sometimes develop around a company to the extent that it becomes a darling of the stock exchange, unable to do wrong. Driven by the consensus of opinion, investors duly plough money in, only to discover later that the consensus did not tally with the true facts of the situation.

How OPM Leasing enmeshed some of America's leading banks and investment bankers readily demonstrates the point.[28] The executives deliberately associated their company with blue–chip companies such as the "Big Eight" accounting firms and leading investment houses. By association, the blue–chip image rubbed off on to OPM to such a degree that OPM gained (unjustified) legitimacy in the marketplace and was universally perceived as bigger and better than it actually was.

Consensus that underwriting was a one–way bet certainly appeared to entice many investors into becoming Lloyd's "names" – Lloyd's of London is a leading international insurance market; "names" are members of underwriting syndicates who take no active part in the underwriting business other than to pro-vide the funds for it. Social acceptability was conferred by the likes of entertainer Adam Faith acting as a recruiter for particular syndicates. Disasters such as tanker spills, asbestos claims, and hurricane damage count among the factors which have all com-bined to ruin many of the names. Such is the extent of the finan-cial ruin that self-help groups now exist and the number of new names joining Lloyds is dropping dramatically every year.

By the same token, Laura in our case study in chapter one "rushed in," rather than spending sufficient time collecting data on the opinions and behaviors of others. This information would have guided her own behavior and allowed her to start to influ-ence James effectively.

Pfeffer[29] suggests that public conformance to others' judgments can not only gain us social acceptance – people are more attracted to those similar to themselves – but also increases our feelings of security.[30] It also minimizes the amount of information searching we have to do for ourselves in unfamiliar situations.[31] In the selec-tion of candidates for interview, for example, if a consensus begins to develop around a particular applicant, it can save a great deal of time on the part of selectors weighing up the individual strengths and weaknesses of individuals. It is rumored that in some of the older English universities, the process of appointment still relies on a consensus of opinion developing around a partic-ular academic, who is then invited to join the institution without any formal process of application.

Organizational life contains so much uncertainty and so much pressure for individuals to make judgments and to take actions under conditions of ambiguity, that the opinions of others can be a very powerful source of influence.[32] And once a consensus of opinion begins to develop, it is very difficult to change. Witness the British Conservative Party's sleaze scandal which broke during 1994, initiated largely by the *Guardian* newspaper's revelations in October 1994 about "cash for questions in parliament." The ensuing furore resulted in the perception of the Conservative Party as sleazy until proven innocent, together with the resignations of several high–profile officeholders.

**RECENT
FINDINGS**

Pfeffer highlights three major implications of the principle of social proof for influencing others at work:[33]

(1) It is absolutely crucial to manage the information environment at work. This can be achieved in a number of ways. Firstly, get in early on any decision making process. Once a consensus begins to develop around a particular issue, it is very difficult to change it, not only because people become committed to that particular position as we saw earlier, but also because the act of agreement makes every individual believe that his or her position is right.

(2) Many managers tend to think that organizational decisions are made rapidly. In actual fact, the principle of social proof suggests that decisions unfold over a period of time as consensus develops. So rather than trying to gain immediate agreement, it is probably better to pursue a strategy which moves people toward a particular view.

(3) It is wise to have the maximum number of allies and supporters to provide you with the social proof and consensus which you need to influence a particular situation. It is essential that you get everyone to take for granted the correctness of your position, and that you are able to cite many others who share your point of view.

■ Principle five: liking and ingratiation

Cialdini reports that we are heavily influenced by, and tend to say "yes" to, those whom we know and like. Liking is used in myriad ways to get us to comply with requests. Cialdini goes on to identify certain key factors upon which liking is based, including:[34]

Social similarity

We tend to like people who resemble us and are from the same social category or group[35] – Tiny Rowland, the merchant adventurer who founded the Lonrho trading empire, cultivated his private–school, upper–class image to ingratiate himself into the British colonial trading class of the African states, for example. Robert Maxwell changed his eastern European name to become more socially acceptable to the British business establishment. Even dress can be important in influencing others to agree with our requests – many organizations actively encourage their employees to project a particular image to the outside world – Coopers and Lybrand, for instance, expects its consultants to wear navy blue or dark grey suits and white shirts or blouses to promote a safe conservative image; similarly, IBM expects its male employees to wear white shirts and navy blue suits.

Physical attractiveness

Attractive people are more liked and likeable[36] – Hillary Clinton dropped the image of the intellectual, feminist lawyer to metamorphose into the glamorously successful wife and mother to influence voters in her husband's favor.

The performance appraisals and salaries of accountants in two firms were studied by Jerry Ross and Kenneth Ferris.[37] They measured the physical attractiveness of the accountants by showing the accountants' pictures to independent outsiders. Their findings revealed that the more physically attractive the accountant, the better the performance appraisal.

Physical attractiveness combined with positive association, and particularly flattery, are very potent weapons in any attempt to influence the behavior of others.

Compliments and flattery

We like those people who like us and who express positive sentiments toward us[38] – Mrs Thatcher was apparently heavily influenced by those ministers such as Cecil Parkinson who lavished compliments upon her.

> One of the more subtle but effective forms of flattery is being responsive and attentive to others.

Compliments and flattery may seem a rather transparent strategy, but consider the dilemma surrounding the rejection of compliments and flattery. If you believe a remark flattering to yourself to be sincere, you will feel positive about yourself and about the person conveying the flattery. If, however, you question the sincerity of the remark, and believe that it had an ulterior motive, you will not feel as good about yourself, you will question the other's opinion of you ("what's wrong with me if others think that I can be so easily taken in by flattery?") and you will not feel positively about the other person. So in a sense, there is a motivational bias for you to believe that any compliment is sincere.

One of the more subtle but effective forms of flattery is being responsive and attentive to others. When this attentiveness is shown by someone who is higher in rank or status, it conveys the flattering impression that your feelings are important enough to concern that person. Think how flattered you feel when somebody superior to you remembers an important detail of your life.

Contacts and cooperation

We tend to like people whom we know well, particularly if we cooperate with them on a common task or toward a common goal, which allows positive feelings to develop. This is clearly identified in the experimental work of the leading social psychologist Muzafer Sherif and his associates.[39] In a boys' summer camp, Sherif and his colleagues first created conflict by letting the boys choose different names for their two groups, by assigning the groups to different residence cabins, and by introducing competitive activity. To bring the two groups back together, the psychologists devised tasks that required cooperation in order to achieve some mutually desirable goal. Successful joint efforts toward common goals steadily bridged the rift between the two groups.

Contact and familiarity can also produce liking – just as we tend to like familiar surroundings, we also tend to like people who are familiar to us. Research from head hunters on senior executive recruitment projects shows that two thirds of senior appointments have an existing point of contact with the company which is recruiting – whether as consultants or via networks developed through joint ventures, conferences, and so on.

Various kinds of pleasure also tend to produce liking – for example, the frequent experience of sharing a pleasant business lunch or a convivial round of golf can evoke feelings of liking as well as the norm of reciprocity.

Association with positive things

We like the bearers of good news and dislike the messengers of bad.[40] Margaret Thatcher was considered to hold Lord Young as her favorite businessman because he always brought the solutions, and not the problems.

The liking and ingratiation principle has multiple implications for influencing others in the flatter organizations of the 1990s, where persuasion, not hierarchy, is more critical in the exercise of power.

Pfeffer[41] argues that the most significant implication is that managers who are warmer and more empathetic will have an easier time influencing others than the tough, macho manager.

He argues that the next in importance is the need to build up networks of supporters and allies who can stand guarantee for you in front of others less close to you.

The principle of liking and ingratiation also highlights the importance of having a good understanding of yourself so that you can begin to work on presenting an image and on employing ingratiation techniques which will successfully influence your target.

In addition, the principle accentuates the importance of assessing your target accurately so that you press the correct buttons to influence successfully.

If you build on one or more of these bases for liking, you are guaranteed to have a strong platform for interpersonal influence.

■ Principle six: emotion

Pfeffer stresses that our hearts influence us every bit as much as our heads. He notes three specific points about the importance of emotions as an influencing technique.[42]

Firstly, it is possible to manage the emotions displayed to others. He cites *The Managed Heart*,[43] in which Arlie Hochschild provides numerous example of organizations such as Delta Airlines which use certain expressed emotions as criteria for employee selection. Delta wants employees who can keep their smile intact throughout a 15–hour flight or during turbulence. Similarly, Disney World not only selects employees of a naturally positive disposition, it also trains them hard to demonstrate sustained outward happiness – "Have a nice day" is a way of life.[44] Watch the newscaster on your TV station tonight and see how he or she matches facial expression to suit the news item – sombre for a plane crash, smiling for a royal engagement.

Secondly, other people's behavior can partly depend on the emotions which we display: in other words, we can manage our heart to influence others' behavior. For example, Tidd and Lockard studied the effect of smiling on the tips earned by a cocktail waitress who served 48 male and 48 female customers.[45] Although the number of drinks ordered was not affected by smiling, the amount of tips earned was as follows: broad smiles generated over $20 in tips, while tight lips earned the waitress less than $10.

Thirdly, the skill to use emotions tactically can be learned or acquired. It obviously requires a tremendous amount of self– control and restraint, not to mention a keen awareness of what you want to achieve and with whom. Many business executives have trained themselves to become experts at concealing their true emotional feelings. President Reagan was an excellent manipulator of emotions in the mass media, as were President Nixon and the Australian prime minister, Bob Hawke – indeed the ability of Nixon and Hawke to manufacture tears for television became legendary. Margaret Thatcher employed the services of ex–Mars marketing man, Gordon Reece, to groom her public image.

What are the implications of the use of emotions as a principle for influencing others? Pfeffer identifies two in particular. Firstly, emotions offer you the potential to ingratiate yourself into the positive feelings or goodwill of others. People are more likely to feel more able to say "yes" to those they feel have made an effort to be pleasant.

Secondly, concealing emotions is vitally important in any negotiation, particularly where to reveal them would be to reveal to the opposition crucial unspoken insights into the importance of particular issues.

The success of any managerial strategy to exercise influence will be determined by the dynamics and synergy of these six principles.

CHAPTER SUMMARY

- This chapter has focussed on understanding the process of influence. It has examined the complex relationship between power and influence.

- The *seven power levers* open to all managers have been identified as resources, information, expertise, connections, coercion, position, and personal power.

- The *six principles of influence* through which managers can activate power were highlighted as contrast, historical commitments and consistency, scarcity, social proof, liking and ingratiation, and emotion.

- We have also seen that the successful application of the principles of influence means that managers may successfully activate power and get things done in the modern, interdependent organization.

CONCEPT QUIZ

Do you understand how to influence effectively and unleash the sources of power available to you?

1. It doesn't pay to flatter your colleagues in interdependent organizations. *True or false?*

2. Managers' power and influence are dependent on their position. *True or false?*

3. Managers unleash power through influencing effectively. *True or false?*

4. Managers can be influential without power. *True or false?*

5. There are at least seven sources of organizational power available to managers. *True or false?*

6. Using your influence is all about the application of social and interpersonal tactics. *True or false?*

7. Influence is coercive and unsubtle. *True or false?*

8. Managers always evaluate proposals on their intrinsic merits, rather than by comparing them with other proposals that they may have recently experienced and any previous commitments they may have made. *True or false?*

9. Interpersonal factors, such as how other colleagues behave, what they think, and who they like, never influence a manager's ability to objectively evaluate proposals. *True or false?*

10. We are all influenced by our hearts as well as our heads. *True or false?*

Answers

1(F), 2(F), 3(T), 4(F), 5(T), 6(T), 7(F), 8(F), 9(F), 10(T).

A PROBLEM OF POWER AND INFLUENCE

Although Laura had failed to win recognition from James for the substantial increase in profitable market share during her first 18 months at the company, she was determined to forge ahead.

She believed that by implementing the initiatives she had identified as paramount to the further growth of market share, she would eventually win James over. Nothing should be able to stop her – after all, she now had the title and thus the authority which she had always wanted.

Laura identified a number of key projects. One such project was a high–profile, tightly targeted public relations campaign to increase brand awareness. To implement the campaign, Laura needed a sophisticated, commercially aware PR Manager.

The incumbent PR Manager, Frank Sykes, was from the old school who believed that hitting targets was what you did with your trade press cronies on a clay pigeon shoot, with less success after lunch than before. The contemporary world of readership profiles, "advertorials," and exclusives was completely alien to him. Employed by the company for over 25 years, Frank had neither the interest nor the ability to embrace this new role. In fact, he freely admitted this to Laura.

Laura decided that Frank was too costly a passenger to keep in his current role and that if he could not rise to the new challenges, then Laura would unfortunately have no choice but to make him redundant.

At the next meeting with James, Laura presented all the objective, commercial reasons for the new role and for Frank's likely redundancy. Much to Laura's surprise, James seemed somewhat reluctant to agree to the recommendation, arguing that Frank had served with him in the navy and that the outstanding loyalty Frank had demonstrated to the flag was now being shown to the company. James closed the meeting abruptly.

At their next meeting, James informed Laura that the company was a caring organization which did not throw long–standing employees overboard at the first sign of trouble. James warned Laura not to raise the issue of Sykes's redundancy again.

Laura was staggered by her failure to get agreement to her proposal. She felt that as marketing director, her recommendations should have been endorsed by her managing director – after all, her proposals were based on thorough, commercial analysis and they did focus on the best interests of the company. And Sykes himself had admitted that he was not up to the new responsibilities.

Review questions

1. Where did Laura go wrong?

2. How could Laura have used her influence to unleash the power levers available to her to gain James's agreement to make Sykes redundant?

SUMMARY CHECKLIST

❏ Identify the people with whom you are interdependent.

❏ Avoid relying only on the authority of position.

❏ Identify the power levers available to you.

❏ Activate power through the process of influencing others.

❏ Influence by managing the context in which proposals are presented.

❏ Influence by managing your own actions and those of others on an inter-personal level.

ACTION CHECKLIST

1. Review how you currently attempt to gain approval for a proposal from those upon whose agreement you depend.

_____

_____

2. Reflect on the kind of thoughts you experience when your proposal is turned down.

_____

_____

3. Identify a proposal which will enable you to practice using the principles of power and influence discussed in this chapter.

_____

_____

4. Identify the people on whom you depend to get the proposal successfully implemented.

_____

_____

5. Develop a list of the possible sources of power available to you to get this proposal implemented.

_____

_____

6. Research the context in which you will present your proposal, so that you can effectively frame it to meet the needs of the situation which you face – what will your proposal be compared to, what previous commitments have been made, and how will it be valued?

_____

_____

7. Begin to build a consensus of opinion amongst colleagues which is supportive of your proposal.

_____

_____

8. Attempt to get liked by, and ingratiate yourself to, the key decision makers.

_____

_____

9. Practice concealing and controlling your range of emotions, and present only those which help you to achieve your objectives.

_____

_____

10. Present your proposal and then review how successful your first attempt to consciously influence has been.

_____

_____

chapter three

STEP ONE – KNOW YOURSELF

This chapter focuses on the relationship between self-awareness and successful influencing. It shows how beliefs, values, assumptions, and styles of interpersonal behavior all affect your ability to influence others to agree to your goals. It argues that you should consciously manage these elements in order to control and manipulate the range of impressions you make on the people you meet and need to influence.

The chapter highlights that you must be clear on exactly what you want to achieve, in order to capitalize fully on your control of a wide repertoire of impressions. To focus on your goal, you must learn to put emotions to one side.

Flexibility in how you reach that focussed longer-term goal is shown to be vital, particularly the ability to submerge your own ego in order to play the nonthreatening, backroom boy in the short term.

The chapter ends with a discussion of how personal energy, physical stamina, and mental perseverance are all critical to the successful exercise of influence.

SELF-ASSESSMENT EXERCISE

How do you make things happen?

The self-assessment exercise offers a useful means to understand yourself and how your assumptions, beliefs, and attitudes may affect your ability to influence effectively. The exercise explores the factors which you believe to be important in getting things done and making things happen within organizations.

For each of the following statements, circle the number which most closely resembles your attitude.

Statement	Disagree			Agree	
	a lot	a little	neutral	a little	a lot
1. The best way to handle people is to tell them what they want to hear.	1	2	3	4	5
2. When you ask someone to do something for you, it is best to give the real reason for wanting it, rather than reasons which might carry more weight.	1	2	3	4	5
3. Anyone who completely trusts someone else is asking for trouble.	1	2	3	4	5
4. It is hard to get ahead without cutting corners here and there.	1	2	3	4	5
5. It is safest to assume that all people have a vicious streak, and it will come out when they are given a chance.	1	2	3	4	5
6. One should take action only when it is morally right.	1	2	3	4	5
7. Most people are basically good and kind.	1	2	3	4	5
8. There is no excuse for lying to someone else.	1	2	3	4	5
9. Most people forget more easily the death of their father than the loss of their property.	1	2	3	4	5
10. Generally speaking, most people won't work hard unless forced to do so.	1	2	3	4	5

To obtain your score, add up the numbers you circled for questions 1, 3, 4, 5, 9, and 10. For the other four questions, reverse the numbers you have circled, so that 5 becomes 1, 4 becomes 2, 2 becomes 4, and 1 becomes 5. Then total both sets of numbers to find your score.

The assumption scores indicate your beliefs about the relative importance of the various factors which make things happen and get things done in organizations.

The lower the score (i.e. below 25), the more likely you are to assume and believe that demonstrating such humane qualities as openness, trust, objectivity, and support in relationships with others improves managerial effectiveness.

The higher the score (i.e above 25), the more pragmatic your behavior, the firmer your belief that manipulation and maneuver are essential to achievement, the greater your emotional control and emotional distance, and the stronger your conviction that the ends justify the means.

When you have calculated your score, answer the following questions:

1. Identify a situation where your style of getting something done proved to be ineffective because your assumptions about how to make things happen in organizations were wrong.

   _____

   _____

   _____

   _____

   _____

   _____

2. Analyze why your approach did not work. Did you make incorrect assumptions about what was important to your target, for example? Did you fail to make a good impression? Did you have an unclear goal?

   _____

   _____

   _____

   _____

   _____

   _____

3. What other styles of behavior could you have used to influence your target?

_____

_____

_____

_____

_____

_____

Source: R. Christie and F.L. Geis, _Studies in Machiavellianism._ © Academic Press, 1970. Reprinted by permission of the authors and publisher. As adapted in _Training in Interpersonal Skills_ by Robbins, Stephen, © 1989. Adapted by permission of Prentice-Hall, Inc., Upper Saddle River, NJ.

Follow-up

This activity is designed to help you analyze what your beliefs, values, and assumptions are, and how they impact on the style which you adopt to influence in your job. You will probably feel that your style works in some situations, but positively hinders you in others.

What the exercise will certainly demonstrate is that you need to become conscious of your style of interpersonal behavior so that you can take control of the impression you make on the people you meet and need to influence.

Plugging into influence

Who are you, and what impression do you create?

To become influential, you must know who you are and, just as importantly, what your beliefs, values, and assumptions are. Beliefs, values, and assumptions determine our style, our behavior, and our attitudes about the right way of doing things. They shape the kind of impressions we unconsciously present to others when we try to influence them.

Most people are not very good at examining their basic beliefs and assumptions – this often makes it hard to understand why these very beliefs may actually be hindering attempts to use influence. But by the same token, learning how to diagnose beliefs, values, and assumptions can unlock previously unknown resources and increase the repertoire of styles and strategies for influencing others.

A good example of softening a personal style while still facing up to tough decisions is provided by Roger Smith, chief executive officer of General Motors. As he expressed it to *Business Week* magazine:

> "I sat down and figured out that, for the good of the corporation, I was going to have to change the way I did things. I used to just make up my mind to do something and to tell somebody that's the way I wanted it done. Now I sit down and we make Team Decisions. ... I spend a lot more time working at participative management. But I have to admit we get better decisions out of it."[1]

> Learning how to diagnose beliefs, values, and assumptions can unlock previously unknown resources and increase the repertoire of styles and strategies for influencing others.

In other words, Roger Smith had to reexamine his beliefs, assumptions, and attitudes about the right way of doing things in order to become more successful in influencing others.

How do beliefs, values, and assumptions impact on our success at influencing others to gain agreement to our goals?

We exhibit our values and attitudes by our unconscious styles of interpersonal behavior. That is not to say, however, that our unconscious styles of behavior are necessarily the most effective for a given situation. Conscious management of our style of interpersonal behavior can allow us actively to control the impressions we make.

The respected sociologist, Erving Goffman, dubs this process of conscious impression management as "the presentation of self in everyday life."[2] Professor Goffman regards our behavior in everyday meetings as performances which have many similarities to theatrical performances. Unlike the stage performer, however, the influencer's job is to project and sustain a particular impression based on the goal he or she wishes to achieve which then influences the target to comply with the influencer's request. Goffman describes this as "defining the situation."[3]

> The key message for the successful use of influence, therefore, is to become conscious of the impressions you are projecting and know what part or style to use with what person and under what circumstances.

Professor Goffman views all interactions as "performance:"

> **"A 'performance' may be defined as all the activity of a given participant on a given occasion which serves to influence in any way any of the other participants."[4] He sees individuals as playing "parts" and "routines" during these performances in order to achieve influence in a given social situation.[5]**

DEFINITION

The key message for the successful use of influence, therefore, is to become conscious of the impressions you are projecting and to know which part or style to use with what person and under what circumstances. Truly successful influencers match their style of behavior (what psychologists call "projected self-image") to the target's perceived self-image.

Sir Bernard Ingham, the longest serving press secretary to a British prime minister, offers a master class in this matching process. This bluff Yorkshireman with a "volcanic temperament" exerted enormous influence on prime minister Margaret

Thatcher by carefully aligning his projected self-image to her perceived self-image.[6] She saw herself as a "can do" politician, and so she wanted to be surrounded by men and women who would give her the "can do" message. Rather than offer her the traditional civil service message of "it can't be done," Ingham played Thatcher's perceived self-image straight back to her:

> "Bernard Ingham was one of the first of the 'can do' civil servants around her. For all his bluffness, Ingham had sensitively attuned antennae, though at times these do seem to be protruding from a human bulldozer. It did not take his antennae long to pick up precisely what Margaret Thatcher was about as a politician."[7]

Formal academic studies have reinforced this finding that sensitivity to the ways others present themselves and the subsequent use of such insight to adjust self-presentation strategies, can dramatically improve performance in jobs where communication with many people is necessary.[8] This research suggests that impression management is particularly important in the flatter organizations of the 1990s where persuasion is critical to a manager's ability to get things done.

Interviewed in the *Harvard Business Review*, Lawrence A. Bossidy, chairman and chief executive of Allied Signal (the $13 billion industrial supplier of aerospace systems, automotive parts, and chemical products), argues that the best people are those who are the best communicators and persuaders, and who have an intrinsic interest in people issues:

> "Today's corporation is a far cry from the old authoritarian vertical hierarchy I grew up in. The cross-functional ties among individuals and groups are increasingly important. They're channels of activity and communication. The traditional bases of managerial authority are eroding. In the past, we used to reward the lone rangers in the corner offices because their achievements were brilliant even though their behavior was destructive. That day is gone. We need people who are better at persuading than at barking orders, who know how to coach and build consensus. Today, managers add value by brokering

with people, not by presiding over empires. That has a big impact on how you think about who the 'best' people are.

"Don't get me wrong. We're not looking for back-slapping nice guys. ... Competition is tough, and it takes brains to win. But today we look for smart people with an added dimension: they have an interest in other people and derive psychic satisfaction from working with them."[9]

It is quite possible that presenting a particular kind of impression may require you to totally reassess your particular set of beliefs, values, and attitudes. You might then decide that the cost is too great and that a particular influence goal is not worth pursuing. Take the Princess of Wales as an example: in an interview in 1995 for the BBC TV program *Panorama*, the Princess revealed to 24 million viewers worldwide that the cost of projecting the image of a fairy-tale marriage on the public stage was just too great – so much so that she had been driven to attempt suicide. In other words, Princess Diana had decided that inclusion in the royal family – the "firm" – was just not worth the sacrifice of her values, the denial of her true self.

Another important aspect of successful impression management is the ability to avoid being perceived as "acting," as just "putting it on." To be successful, how you present yourself should match how others perceive your true self.[10] We can draw on the example of Margaret Thatcher in the run-up to her 1979 election victory to illustrate the concept:

> "Suddenly, it was presentationally useful to have a woman Leader of the Opposition who had a deep hatred of inflation, while the Labour Government was presiding over runaway prices. All she had to do was to behave in public like the housewife she is in private. Similarly, with the soaring bill for public expenditure, she had merely to allude to the housewife's need to budget and she was scoring political points that few men in Britain could hope to achieve."[11]

Congruence between image and "true self" can be obtained either by modifying the image or, less frequently perhaps, by modifying the "true self." Margaret Thatcher did both, as her constituency agent and biographer Andrew Thomson reveals:

"She is aware – perhaps more so as a woman Prime Minister than most men – just how much she is a 'product' that needs to be marketed and sold. It was not unusual, therefore, for Margaret Thatcher to question, not for the first time, whether she was projecting the right 'personal' image. Comparison of photographs of her taken in 1975 when she became Conservative Party Leader with those taken during and after the 1979 General Election tell the story. She had her teeth capped. She changed her hairstyle, a decision that seems to have been hers alone, to give it a gentler line, removing a certain harshness that had existed before. She moderated her tone of voice too. ... She repeats the exercise from time to time, as, before the 1987 General Election, she called in an outside adviser to discuss clothes and her image."[12]

But her "true self" also required modification – Thomson writes that when she became prime minister: "... she was at times almost frozen in those early months in Number 10 between the paralysing forces of a Civil Service and a Cabinet each seeking to impose its will."[13]

Bernard Ingham, her impression manager extraordinaire, came to the rescue:

"... Ingham took the essence of Margaret Thatcher out to the media. He scoffed at the idea of U-turns. He disparaged faint-hearts in the Cabinet. A crisis over proposals to cut planned rises in Government spending? Ministers would just have to find the cuts or she would sort them out. Listening to Ingham gave the media the certain impression that there was a ferocious tigress on the loose in Whitehall. The image seemed to shriek that if anyone unwarily crossed her path, she would kill as soon as look at them. ... It was not until she had been in office for three years that she began to operate fully in accordance with the image."[14]

Richard Branson of the multimillion pound Virgin empire is an outstanding business example of someone who has very perceptively projected an impression which is entirely consistent with what people perceive to be his true self – in other words, his image is plausible, there is nothing to see through. His open-collar style, his woolly sweaters, his unassuming voice, together with the nonhierarchical nature of the business empire run from his own Notting Hill home and Maida Vale houseboat, have all projected an approach to business full of integrity and for the good of the common man.[15] He has pursued this image with vigor:

> "Virgin had, to a large extent, been built on Branson's abilities at man-management and manipulation. ... The atmosphere of almost wilful asceticism – a stoic sense of 'doing without' – that permeated the company grew unconsciously from Branson himself. His almost total indifference to the trappings of conspicuous wealth or consumption proved a subtle, yet powerful, role-model, and a disincentive to the usual gripes about status and salary. Virgin took its tone from Richard's unkempt appearance, his apparent indifference to material luxuries, the fact that his money went not towards Savile Row suits or extravagant limousines but back into the company. If Richard drove a beaten-up car, it seemed that nobody could reasonably ask for anything more themselves."[16]

It was the same impression that was to mislead Lord King when chairman of British Airways into totally underestimating Branson when the latter entered the international airline business in 1983 with Virgin Atlantic. As Lord King subsequently commented:

> "If Richard Branson had worn a pair of steel-rimmed glasses and shaved off his beard, I would have taken him seriously."[17]

When the projected impression moves too far away from what is perceived as the true self, impression management breaks down. American First Lady, Hillary Clinton, offers an insight into this process. To help win votes for her husband to become President, she transformed herself from ardent feminist, bespectacled lawyer into glamorous well-groomed career woman. The majority of the electorate and political commentators found this metamorphosis acceptable, and judged it to be relatively close to Hillary Clinton's true self. To counter subsequent criticism that President Clinton was merely Hillary's husband, the First Lady then metamorphosed into a supportive wife and mother role, complete with subdued clothing. Given her strident background, in general, and her attempts at health reform, in particular, this new image was seen as an unbelievable "act." Her ability to influence was diminished accordingly. Contrast her attempted projection as the archetypal mother and wife with that of her predecessor Barbara Bush, matronly enough to be perceived as George Bush's mother!

Many managers experience considerable difficulty, however, in understanding themselves and in managing the impressions which they create. In chapter one, we exploded the myth of the expertise-oriented, cerebral, and analytical manager. We also discussed the need for softer, intuitive, and insightful skills.

The evidence suggests that a full 68 percent of first-line managers still fall into the cerebral/analytical category, as well as 47 percent of senior managers.[18] These managers are simply not interested in their own behavior or that of others – they feel that objective technical facts, rather than the subjective norms, values, and behavior of others should guide behavior. But this management myopia will hinder their ultimate success.

In our case study, for instance, Laura's lack of self-understanding stopped her from presenting herself in the best possible light and from choosing an influence strategy appropriate to the needs of James, the managing director. Why? Laura assumed that James was influenced by rationality and by the power of expertise. Accordingly, Laura used rational criteria to flag up that she wished to become managing director. Had she been more critically aware of the person and circumstances she was facing, Laura might have been more successful playing the backroom person.

First steps in self-education

Systematic impression management

You should aim to have a broad repertoire of styles for dealing with people to achieve your influence goals. Relying on merely one or two styles of dealing with people will deliver success in some instances, but cannot guarantee to consistently deliver success in all cases. For most of us, using a wide range of behaviors does not come easily because we tend to rely on the one or two approaches which have worked for us in the past.

The self-assessment exercise which you completed at the beginning of the chapter will have helped you to identify the approaches upon which you rely most heavily and which have served you well in the past. These approaches will almost certainly not work across the complete range of situations which you will encounter in everyday working life in the flat, interdependent organizations of the 1990s.

How do you begin to develop and manage the range of impressions you wish to convey in order to influence your target? In the first place, you must start to plan consciously and systematically how you are going to interact with others. This systematic planning involves developing a positive self-image and a clear understanding of the processes involved in impression management.

■ Developing a positive self-image

A positive self-image is a vital prerequisite for successful impression management because it will allow you to feel confident that when you enter an interaction, you will handle it well. This confidence represents the celebrated "I'm OK view."[19]

Maureen Guirdham describes your self-image as the mental picture of yourself which describes the sort of person you think you really are.[20] There are two dimensions to your self-image: an actual/ideal dimension and a private/social dimension. These dimensions combine to give four facets of self-image as shown below.[21]

Figure 2
Four facets of self-image

	Actual self-image	*Ideal self-image*
Private self	How I actually see myself	How I would ideally like to see myself
Social self	How I believe others see me	How I would ideally like others to see me

(Reproduced by permission of the publisher from Maureen Guirdham, Interpersonal Skills at Work, *Prentice Hall, 1990)*

There may well be some discrepancy between the actual and the ideal of your private and social self-images. This is acceptable provided the discrepancy is marginal and results from the desire to improve and to continue learning.[22]

The problems start, Guirdham argues, when the discrepancy is too extreme.[23] Too great a negative discrepancy between the actual and the ideal – in other words, low self-esteem – will prevent you achieving your goals. You will be held back from asking for what you want; you may avoid confronting particular people or situations; and your self-concept may prove self-fulfilling because others perceive you as you perceive yourself.

> There are two dimensions to your self-image: an actual/ideal dimension and a private/social dimension.

Being at the other extreme of the scale is just as bad. By overvaluing yourself, for example, you may commit disastrous social errors and mistakes, such as failing to listen to another person's views.

The keys to positive self-image are thinking and behaving positively.

■ Understanding the elements involved in impression management

Having started to develop a positive self-image, you can then consciously begin to manage the impressions you wish to convey to your influence target. Successful management of this process requires a clear understanding of the different elements illustrated below.

> The first objective in any influence attempt is to ensure that you project an appropriate, clear definition of the situation and that your behavior supports this definition.

Figure 3
Elements in Impression Management

- Define the situation.

- Decide the opening gambit.

- Maintain face.

- Be tactful – allow others to maintain face.

- Manage how much information you convey.

- Manage the level and type of contact with the target.

- Take small steps.

- Introduce some ambiguity.

(Based on Goffman's *Presentation of Self in Everyday Life*)

Define the situation

As Goffman argued, our everyday meetings with other people are designed to sustain a particular definition of a situation.[24] So the first objective in any influence attempt is to ensure that you project an appropriate, clear definition of the situation and that your behavior supports this definition. At a job interview, for instance, your behavior will focus on making an implicit statement about the ideal fit which you provide to the job on offer.

Decide the opening gambit

You must be absolutely clear on what basis the interaction is taking place.[25] Keeping with the example of our job interview, the candidate's opening remarks will suggest whether the candidate views the interviewer as an equal, as a superior, or as a subordinate. If you project yourself in a fashion unacceptable to the other person, the process will collapse. A senior manager interviewing an eighteen-year-old fresh out of school, for example, will not be impressed by being treated as an equal.

Maintain face

To project and then sustain a particular definition of a given situation requires the ability to maintain face. Face means the image we project to our audience, the outside world.[26]

Back in the interview room, our candidate will maintain face – that is, project the image of a perfect match for the job – by highlighting the positive elements of fit and by suppressing elements which do not support the argument.

On the world stage, Boris Yeltsin, President of Russia, provides an example of the dangers of losing face, of letting the mask slip and exposing a projected image as just an act. Yeltsin worked hard to create an image for himself as leader of a world superpower, only to let the mask slip by appearing drunk during a state visit to Germany and by failing to disembark from an aeroplane on a formal stopover to Ireland, apparently because of in-flight overindulgence.

Be tactful – allow others to maintain face

Many managers who have a high-expertise orientation are often somewhat scornful of the contributions made by less informed colleagues, whether these colleagues are of a higher, similar, or junior social level. These scornful managers are often regarded as rather tactless and too task-oriented. In other words, they forego the opportunity to use influence effectively because they deprive others of the ability to maintain or save face.[27] Without tact, you will never influence others effectively.

President Clinton showed his mastery at impression management during his 1995 visit to Northern Ireland when he constantly made eye contact with all the members of the public whom he met and maintained an unswerving interest in what they had to say. In other words, he allowed the man in the street to preserve an image of individual importance in the peace process.

In the example cited above of President Yeltsin's inability to disembark and meet the Irish dignitaries (who were waiting patiently outside the plane), the Irish political establishment nevertheless allowed Yeltsin to maintain face by putting it about that Yeltsin was physically exhausted by his previous trip to the States. For the Irish, telling it how it really was would have achieved nothing.

> Without tact, you will never influence others effectively.

Manage how much information you convey

By regulating the volume of information you convey, you can control your own impressions much more successfully.

Richard Branson is masterful at controlling how much information he gives out in business meetings and uses this tactic to generate information about the intentions of his business opponents:

> "Branson became adept at bluff. By the judicious application of nods, grunts and pregnant silences, he could convey the impression that he knew far more than he actually did, whether the conversation was about who had recorded what or what exactly the copyright laws were pertaining to releases in Germany. It bought him time in striking deals with more practised negotiators, while he learnt what was valuable and what was not, what could be surrendered and what must be fought for, at almost any cost."[28]

In contrast, Gerald Ratner, the value-for-money jeweler for the youth market, declared to the outside world that "a prawn sandwich from Marks and Spencer would outlast any product from [his] store." In so doing, Ratner destroyed his eponymous company in the course of one unguarded, after-dinner speech.

Manage the level and type of contact with the target

Bill Clinton demonstrated his awareness of the importance of this type of control on his 1995 Irish peace mission. In his attempt to build immediate empathy, he made his first port of call a factory where he met the men on the shopfloor in their overalls. Similarly, he defused a potentially explosive first public handshake with Gerry Adams by effecting a preplanned, but apparently chance meeting with Adams as the latter left a café.

In the business world, if you talk too openly or too frequently with specific people, you run the risk of losing authority and independence. As Dennis Thatcher so memorably put it: "Whales only get harpooned when they spout."

Take small steps

Most interactions pass through a number of stages – think of a phone call when you start off with small talk before moving to the main topic and then closing, for example, or the social chit-chat which breaks the ice at a business meeting, or the "how was the journey?" at a job interview. But managing the movement between the stages without feeling awkward requires conscious practice.

The underlying reason for feeling awkward is that you are redefining the situation, which in turn involves some renegotiation of the agreement into which you entered with the other party.

The way to manage this is by taking small steps at a time. Imagine a situation where a boy wants to invite a girl out. Rather than being upfront and asking "Would you like to come to Saturday's concert with me?," he might ask if she had heard about the concert – if she replies "Yes, and I was hoping to go," he then has the opportunity to offer to buy tickets for both of them.

Introduce some ambiguity

It often pays to introduce ambiguity into a situation when you are unfamiliar with your influence target or unsure about the target's reaction to your proposal. By hinting at what you are suggesting, rather than making an explicit request or invitation, you avoid the risk of losing face if your request is turned down.

In our case study, for instance, Laura could have broached the issue of Sykes's possible redundancy with James by reporting that "Some people have suggested to me that Sykes is struggling in his role as public relations manager, but ..." Had James replied, "I'm sure you will agree that Sykes deserves all our support," Laura could then have confirmed that, "Yes, I think he's a good man and I'm happy to work with him to overcome any problems he may be having." By referring to "some people," Laura would have distanced herself from the situation; the ambiguity introduced by her "but ..." would have similarly saved her face. Conversely, had James accepted Laura's feedback on Sykes, then both parties would have conveniently ignored it.

■ Breakdowns in impression management

The successful influencer should always be aware of the potential problems which can interfere with successful impression management.[29]

A wandering mind

How often have you been talking to your influence target and found your mind wandering away to other issues while you lose concentration? Such external preoccupation is a clear signal to your target that the impression you are conveying is compatible neither with what you are thinking, nor with your real regard for that person.

If you have worked on creating an impression of interest in your target, you must sustain this, whatever the circumstances. When the future company president of E. F. Hutton, George Ball, was working for its brokerage division, he developed a strong powerbase through his assiduous attention to all of his staff. He remembered every small detail of their lives and sustained this impression of interest whatever the circumstances:

> "'George had an uncanny ability to remember everything about you,' says a former Hutton account executive. 'He charmed you, he flattered you, he made you feel special. A few years after meeting George for the first time, I bumped into him at a sales meeting. Because I was sure he wouldn't recognize me, I headed over to re-introduce myself. But there was no need for that. No sooner does George spot me than he's shaking my hand, saying, "Hi, how's Betsy and the kids?""'[30]

Too interpersonally aware

Being overly self-conscious will make you nervous and awkward – you will almost certainly lose face, particularly if you are trying to convey an impression of interest in the subject matter.

This often happens when you are overconscious of the status of the other person or if you are sexually attracted to him or her. This can often manifest itself through mistakes in timing (two people go to speak simultaneously, for example) or through talking too fast (this is the "forget to engage brain before speaking" syndrome).

Robert Maxwell had an innovative way of avoiding intimidation by others' greater status: "'When I am confronted by powerful people,' he was fond of explaining, 'I remind myself that all men use lavatory paper.'"[31]

If you are simultaneously self-conscious and overconscious of the other person, this exacerbates your problems by making you overconscious of the whole interaction process itself.

All of these problems result from a lack of skill, and, more fundamentally, from a lack of emotional self-discipline. Impression management requires you to control your emotions, rather than letting them control you. We will return to emotional control in our consideration of some of the other important factors which you have to master within yourself if you are to succeed at impression management. Let us now turn to a consideration of these factors.

What do you want to achieve?

Part of self-awareness is establishing clearly what goals you wish to achieve. Impressions can then be managed to achieve those particular influence goals. If you look back over history, all of the great influencers have tended to focus on a specific goal. This focus avoids wasting the limited energy at your disposal on unnecessary tasks.[32]

Focusing on one particular goal is easier said than done. It is unusual for an influence attempt to have only one goal – the skill comes in prioritising the multiplicity of goals which will almost certainly exist in real life.

Consider Lyndon Johnson's quest for the Presidency of the United States.[33] The financial hardship he endured as a youth made him crave financial security. An opportunity to make serious money arose when he was invited to participate in a highly attractive oil deal in the early 1940s. He was a Democratic senator for Texas in the US Congress at the time. He turned the deal down. In no way would links with the oil industry have hindered his reelection as a senator in oil-rich Texas: long-term, however, such links would certainly have damaged him when he chose to run for the Presidency. In other words, Johnson's single-minded focus on the primary goal of the Presidency allowed him to subordinate his secondary goal of financial security to it.

John Kotter reports the same principle in the business area,

revealing that successful general managers tended to have con-
centrated their efforts in single companies in the same industrial
sector. Focusing their effort on specific sectoral issues gave huge
depth to their expertise.[34]

Another reason why focusing on your goals is easier said than
done is that emotions are often tangled up with, or invested in,
certain projects or aspects of your work. Personal pride, loyalty,
and large investments of personal time often then blur the
required focus.[35]

The key to emotions is to recognize them and accept that they
are legitimate, but also to use them positively to enhance your
ability to set goals. You can start out by sorting the personal issues
from the larger goal.

Mario Puzo's fictional godfather offers a striking example of an
individual with powerful emotions concerning the protection and
enhancement of his family business interests. The godfather never
let these emotions deflect him from the achievement of his main
goal, however. Instead, he channeled his emotions and took business decisions which may have had some emotionally painful
short-term consequences, but which ultimately served to enhance
his power base. His expertise at focusing on the vital business goal
is summed up by his much-repeated watchword: "It's nothing
personal, it's only business."[36]

The power of previous commitments and the enormous personal investment which they represent have already been discussed. Successful influencers have to be fully aware
of these issues and in some situations, be able to let
go of a project in which they have a large personal
and emotional investment, for the sake of greater
power in the longer term. John Redwood's resigna-
tion in 1995 from the British Conservative Cabinet
lost him immediate ministerial power, but strengthened his
longer-term claim to the leadership of the right-wing of the Conservative Party, completely outflanking the then heir apparent,
Michael Portillo.

> The key to emotions is to recognize them and accept that they are legitimate, but also to use them positively to enhance your ability to set goals.

Richard Branson had a similar ability to let go of projects in which he had made an emotional investment. In September 1981, for example, he established his own magazine to rival the long-established *Time Out*, even though his closest business associates advised against it.[37] Although the initial launch was reasonably successful, things started to go wrong very rapidly. Most importantly, however, Branson was able to let go, even though the affair represented the most public of his business failures:

> "… for Branson a quick death had become preferable to the prospect of a prolonged agony. *Event* had become too much of a drain on both his time and the resources of the rest of the Virgin Group. … The failure of *Event* cost Richard Branson more than £750,000. The cost to his pride was not so easily calculated. He had closed businesses down before, but never so publicly, and the fact that it was a project so dear to his heart wounded even more. … There was nothing for Branson to do now but cut his losses, and trust to a return of the Branson luck."[38]

The need to "let go" is further illustrated by the classic dilemma of the entrepreneur who has the vision to start up a business, but is unable to bring in the professional managers required to develop the business further. This inability to delegate some power stems from the enormous personal commitment which the entrepreneur has made to his "baby." By being focussed on the ultimate goal and by forgetting emotional investments, however, the entrepreneur can succeed and move to the next stage of the business's development.

Bill Gates, the founder of Microsoft, exemplifies this. Running what has become one of the largest software companies in the world while still in his early thirties, Gates is a technical genius with a burning mission to bring the power of computing to the masses. A large degree of his success is due to his unswerving focus on this core goal. As the business has grown, he has had the emotional strength to give up power to the professional managers whom he has brought in to run the business. This route allows him to retain even greater power in the long term.

In an academic study of managers with a high degree of political skill (the "high *Machs*" as compared to the "low *Machs*"), researchers observed that:

> "The dispositional differences between high and low Machs ... are all seen as related consequences of the highs' cool detachment compared to the lows' openness to emotional involvement. ... Although their coolness may not be more than skin-deep, they appear to be thick-skinned enough to withstand the enticements or dangers of interpersonal involvements which might interfere with task achievement."[39]

Indeed, David Montgomery – the hard-nosed Mirror Group chief executive – exemplifies high, cool detachment to the extent that his in-house nickname is "the Iceman."

Attention to detail is another aspect of focus which is critical to building power and influence.[40] As Jim Wright's biographer wrote of Wright's ascent to speaker of the House of Representatives:

> "Minutiae mattered. Members believe one function of the leadership ... is to service them just as they service constituents. Minutiae measured this service. Wright had thrived on minutiae, had proven his willingness to do little things for colleagues, not just on Public Works or on a trip to a district. For years he had learned the names and faces of just-elected members so he could greet them by name. Several members recalled that Wright was the first colleague they met when they arrived in Washington."[41]

Sir Richard Greenbury, chairman of Marks and Spencer, exercises enormous attention to detail. He holds monthly management team meetings at which he individually tastes new additions to the Marks and Spencer range of ready-made meals. His involvement extends to commenting on the ratio of meat to sauce. He also plays an active role in determining each season's color and fashion range.

Philip Harris exemplifies the same trait. In 1977 Harris Carpets acquired the loss-making Queensway Carpets. One of the hall-marks of Harris's subsequent turnaround was his massive attention to detail. For example, he centralized all control systems on himself, making store managers telephone him with trading figures four times a week, including weekends.[42]

Conversely, lack of attention to detail can have dire consequences, as George Davies of retailer Next found out to his cost:

> "I had this great idea – and you can convince a lot of people if you have a great idea – but I'd never run a business in my life before. I didn't know anything about warehousing … about systems, I didn't know that if you didn't file correctly and people have queries, you will never find that again."[43]

The fortunes of the Xerox Corporation in the 1970s also illustrate the dangers of being distracted along the way. Two factors combined to make Xerox chief executive, Peter McClough, lose sight of his grand vision to move beyond the copier business.[44] Not only was he diverted by a time-consuming suit brought by the government for antitrust violations; he also lost focus by becoming involved in many high-profile public activities outside Xerox:

> "He volunteered his own time and effort to the United Way, the University of Rochester Board of Trustees, the Council on Foreign Relations, the US/USSR Trade and Economic Council, the Overseas Development Council, the International Executive Service Corps, the Business Committee for the Arts, the National Urban League, and the United Negro College Fund. In 1968 he was a Humphrey delegate at the Democratic convention in Chicago, in 1972 he co-chaired the national fund raising drive for Democratic congressional candidates, in 1973 he was named treasuer of the Democratic National Party and in 1975 he chaired the commitee exploring Senator Henry Jackson's presidential bid. Peter McClough was involved."[45]

Effort is wasted by being spread too thinly, and details that may be significant in building power and influence may be overlooked.

Flexibility in goal attainment

Being aware of your priority goal is an obvious advantage, but being blinkered as to how to achieve it can be dangerous.[46] Any number of factors can blinker you into thinking that there is only one way to achieve your goal – you may be excited about the idea, or perhaps be highly committed to it. But you must have the all-round vision to identify what other options are open to you to achieve your goal – in short, you need flexibility.

Rosabeth Moss Kanter found that effective managers of change combined dogged persistence with flexibility.[47] Whilst focusing on the end result to which they were committed, these managers employed finesse and flexibility as they negotiated with the various stakeholders whose help they needed. This allowed them to modify the means to match reality, while preserving the integrity of the ultimate goal.

This is well illustrated by looking at the political arena. Achieving power is the only goal – consider the example of Franklin D. Roosevelt whose uncle was President of the United States and whose cousins flooded the Republican Party. Although a Republican both by family and by upbringing, Franklin Roosevelt launched his own bid for the Presidency from within the Democrats, simply because the route was less crowded by siblings.

President Chirac of France altered his political stance to win the presidential elections on the third attempt; cynics might argue that the British Conservative MPs who defected to other parties in 1996 before the elections were motivated as much by job security as by ideology.

Inflexibility can be dangerous – you can be broken if you do not blow with the wind. Archetypal "conviction politician" Margaret Thatcher made for her own downfall precisely because of her proud boasts of "This lady's not for turning" and "There is no alternative." As discussed previously, she persisted with the Poll Tax in the 1980s, despite the national mood of extreme discontent and her colleagues' advice.

Another vital aspect of flexibility is the ability to submerge your ego when the occasion arises, in order to get something accomplished.[48] You might choose to play the backroom boy today to gain greater power and resources tomorrow. Francis Urquhart in the televised political novel *House of Cards*[49] provides an excellent illustration of this. As chief whip in the government of a lame-duck prime minister, Urquhart deliberately plays the backroom boy to the prime minister, apparently putting aside his own personal ambitions in the greater interests of the party. When the prime minister is eventually forced to resign, he puts Urquhart forward as his preferred replacement above the other contenders who had been outspoken about their political ambitions. Right up to the moment of his election to prime minister, Urquhart succeeds in maintaining the impression of a man dragged reluctantly toward the seat of power.

A real-life political example of the dangers of naked ego for long-term success can be found in the successor to Margaret Thatcher. It was the modest backroom boy, John Major, who got the better of the more up-front political contenders such as Michael Heseltine. As Margaret Thatcher noted in her autobiography:

> "John Major was not at first very keen on becoming Foreign Secretary. A modest man, aware of his inexperience, he would probably have preferred a less grand appointment. But I knew that if he was to have a hope of becoming Party leader, it would be better if he had held one of the three great offices of state. ... I had simply concluded that he must be given wider public recognition and greater experience if he was to compete with the talented self-publicists who would be among his rivals."[50]

Can you stand the pace?

We have spent some time helping you to get to know yourself better. This increased self-awareness should allow you to better understand how you interact with others and how you should present yourself to your influence target.

Now that you have expert/technical skills plus interpersonal self-awareness, you must now consider whether you have the energy and physical stamina to follow through successfully on becoming an influential manager.[51]

It may seem strange to highlight energy and physical stamina, but becoming influential requires both endurance and tenacity. How often have you thought to yourself: "I just haven't got the energy to deal with that person's attempt to score points over me – I've so much work to do already?"

Take a long look at the senior managers in your organization and ask yourself: "What is it that makes these people powerful and influential?" Of course it is partly to do with ability, but not exclusively – it is perhaps more about personal drive and physical stamina. Kotter's study of general managers in industry reported that many of them worked 60 or more hours per week, in other words six 10-hour days minimum.[52]

Margaret Thatcher's premiership was marked by her tremendous stamina, endurance, and perseverance. In an era when the pressures and responsibilities of leadership were greater then ever before, Margaret Thatcher defied all of the predictions that she would burn out or collapse:

> "In fact, she gave warning of this extraordinary stamina shortly after she became Prime Minister, when there was widely expressed surprise at her ability to keep working flat out on as little as four hours sleep a night. She said: 'Don't forget, I have been going flat out for twenty years. People think that you wake up one fine day and find yourself Prime Minister, having had a laid-back sort of existence. I have never had a laid-back existence. I have always been immensely busy.'"[53]

Owen Oyston, former chairman and CEO of the Oyston group of companies, summed up his energy levels like this:

> "The biggest single thing really is this driving force and the fact that you cannot relax. I can never relax; seven days a week I have to work.

... I cannot find, nor wish to have, time off to go away and relax and have a holiday. I have to be working ...."[54]

The success of Frank Stanton, president of CBS, was facilitated by his seemingly insatiable appetite for putting in the hours:

> "His idea of relaxation was arriving in the office on Sunday wearing a sports coat. He survived on little sleep, usually five hours a night. ... Stanton was in the office by 7:30 or 8:00 a.m., and by the time everyone else arrived at nine or ten, he was miles ahead."[55]

This physical and emotional staying power allows successful influencers to harness their interpersonal skills to draw people into their web of influence. Working those longer hours in pursuit of influence allows you to outsmart the opposition – whether you are establishing contacts in informal encounters; creating bonds and alliances; collecting insights, gossip, rumours, leaks and personal insights; or exchanging favors.

Is it a coincidence that the Palace of Westminster, a magnet for influencers, boasts over seven bars on the parliamentary estate alone, all open until 2:00 a.m. if necessary, and dedicated to the trade of power and influence?

Such energetic drive also represents a mechanism in itself for increasing your influence: not only does it inspire those around you, it also highlights the significance of the task in hand. Thus, Richard Branson succeeded in inspiring a company atmosphere "of frenetic activity, coupled with extreme informality."[56]

CHAPTER SUMMARY

- This chapter has focussed on the need to understand yourself before you can influence effectively.

- It has shown how beliefs, values, and assumptions affect your success in influencing others to gain agreement to your goals.

- It has argued for the conscious management of your beliefs, values, and assumptions.

- It recommends that you develop various styles of interpersonal behavior in order to control and manipulate the range of impressions you make on the people whom you need to influence.

- Having outlined a repertoire of styles and skills in impression management, the chapter has examined the need to decide what your ultimate goals are, and why you need to separate emotions away from business objectives in order to achieve influencing success.

- The chapter has stressed the need for flexibility in goal attainment, but also the need to submerge your ego to play the backroom boy for the achievement of longer-term goals.

- Finally we have seen that becoming influential requires tremendous energy, physical stamina, and mental perseverance.

CONCEPT QUIZ

Do you understand the relationship between self-understanding and success in influencing others?

1. The impression you create through your behavior is irrelevant in trying to exercise influence. *True or false?*

2. The only way to get the job done is to focus on the task. *True or false?*

3. My hidden thoughts and views can often affect my ability to get others to do what I want them to do. *True or false?*

4. Successful managers have a multiplicity of goals. *True or false?*

5. The way to succeed is to get emotionally involved in a project. *True or false?*

6. Being flexible in the way in which you achieve a particular goal is a sign of weakness. *True or false?*

7. Spending time understanding yourself is a waste of energy. *True or false?*

8. Endurance and perseverance are key attributes of the successful influencer. *True or false?*

9. Always get straight to the point in trying to gain agreement from your influence target. *True or false?*

10. Presenting different impressions to different people is a waste of management time. *True or false?*

Answers

1(F), 2(F), 3(T), 4(F), 5(F), 6(F), 7(F), 8(T), 9(F) and 10(F).

THE FOX EATS THE SHEEP: A PROBLEM OF POLITICAL NAIVETY

Laura's continued hard work delivered an increasing market share for the company. Although her products were now market leaders, Laura still had problems with James. She kept trying to win his approval through the quality of her marketing and general business approach, but all her efforts fell on stony ground.

In fact, James seemed deliberately to devise situations to put Laura down. Over drinks at a national sales conference, for example, he asked Laura for feedback on the product range which he had launched before her appointment – "Tell me straight," he said, "I'd be interested to know."

Laura took James's request as a genuine and rational attempt to tap her expertise to evaluate the company's marketing effectiveness. Accordingly, she suggested that launching an expensive product range without any prior market research was perhaps not the most informed business approach to use in the complex market conditions of the 1990s.

Once Laura had made her contribution, James smiled, nodded wisely and suggested that Laura's response was just what he would have expected from a business-school graduate – all theory and no practice. "Get your hands dirty in the marketplace, get stuck in," he added, "that's the real way to do research." And with that, he moved on to social chit-chat with other members of the management team. Their knowing smiles increased Laura's isolation yet further. Laura felt foolish and humiliated, knowing that she had been led like a lamb to the slaughter by the silver-tongued fox.

When she went home that evening, she explained to Neil her frustration at James's manipulative gameplaying. Neil suggested that there was a mismatch between Laura's view of appropriate business behavior and the view held by James. Neil considered that James must be playing to a different agenda.

Neil advised Laura to take some time out and assess why she was failing to influence James effectively. Perhaps she should reassess what she hoped to get out of this job, bearing in mind the people and circumstances she was confronting. Did Laura honestly think that James was acting as her fatherly mentor, grooming her as his successor? If not, then why not consider managing her current job differently?

Review questions

1. How do you rate Laura's self-awareness and her awareness of others?

2. Explain how Laura could have handled the situation differently?

3. Laura had a clear goal of becoming managing director, but was she handling it correctly?

SUMMARY CHECKLIST

❑ Identify what your values, beliefs, and assumptions are.

❑ Identify how your values and assumptions affect your style of behavior and success in influencing others.

❑ Begin to develop a range of styles through more conscious impression management.

❑ Try out your different styles by starting with relatively easy targets.

❑ Identify what your goals are.

❑ Sort out the personal issues from your ultimate business goal.

❑ Be flexible in the way you achieve your goals.

❑ Develop energy and physical stamina to persevere and follow through.

ACTION CHECKLIST

1. Examine yourself – what are your values and assumptions, and how do these influence the way you behave at work?

_____

_____

2. Identify a situation where your values and assumptions about people have frustrated your attempts to achieve agreement.

_____

_____

3. List the possible alternative strategies you could have used to help you achieve your objective at (2) above. Which of these might have been more successful and why?

_____

_____

4. Identify your career goal.

_____

_____

5. List the range of strategies which you can use to achieve this goal.

_____

_____

6. Leave your personal feelings out of all attempts to achieve your goal.

_____

_____

7. Practice concealing your emotions about a proposal or person by ingratiating yourself to them.

_____

_____

8. Try concealing your true ambitions in the short-term to develop a non-threatening relationship with your boss.

_____

_____

9. Think about how you will attempt to define the situation when you interact with your influence target.

_____

_____

10. Identify any potential problems you may have in trying to sustain the impression you have created.

_____

_____

chapter
four

STEP TWO – IDENTIFY YOUR TARGET

- Self assessment exercise
- Why assess your target?
- Learning to perceive
- The five-stage person-perception process
- Perceptual interpretation errors
- Use multiple indicators
- Chapter summary
- Concept quiz
- Feature case study
- Summary checklist
- Action checklist

This chapter focuses on the need to pick out and analyze which targets are essential for achieving your goals and which are likely to influence what should be done and how.

Targets must be evaluated and managed – this chapter identifies correct interpretation of other people's behavior as a key prerequisite for any successful attempt to exercise influence.

Improved people-perception skills will help you to understand who you are dealing with. These skills will allow your target to feel comfortable with any attempt to voluntarily change his or her attitudes to events, people, and decisions in order that your ideas may be implemented.

We will also focus on some of the breakdowns in correctly perceiving your influence target, such as stereotyping, making negative attributions, and assuming intentionality. The chapter demonstrates how you should gather clues from a variety of sources – verbal and nonverbal signs, organizational factors – in order to avoid such breakdowns in perception.

SELF-ASSESSMENT EXERCISE

Interpreting your target

A good way to start developing your skills at understanding your target is to evaluate the type of cues upon which you draw to evaluate others. Answer "yes" or "no" to each of the following questions:

1. If I want something from someone, I always expect that the person will respond rationally to my request. *Yes or no?*

2. When I want something from someone, I never consider acquiring as much personal information about that person as possible beforehand. *Yes or no?*

3. When I want something from someone, I concentrate on how *I* view things, rather than on how *he* or *she* might see things. *Yes or no?*

4. I always judge a person by his or her accent. *Yes or no?*

5. I avoid maintaining eye contact with the person to whom I am speaking to ensure that the conversation goes well. *Yes or no?*

6. Before presenting a proposal to someone, I tend not to find out details about that person's job and its impact on his or her behavior. *Yes or no?*

7. When I am listening to someone, I pay attention only to that person's words and deliberately ignore the body language. *Yes or no?*

8. Facial expressions are entirely natural and cannot be orchestrated at will. *Yes or no?*

9. I am always able to judge people accurately by the way they look. *Yes or no?*

10. When I want something from someone, I use memos whenever I can, avoiding a face-to-face meeting if at all possible. *Yes or no?*

Scoring key and interpretation

Award yourself 1 point for every "yes" and 0 for "no." A score of 7 or higher suggests that you have difficulty interpreting people. A score of 4, 5, or 6 indicates that you have a significant amount of development work to do in order to understand your target effectively. A score of 3 or less means you are already effective at interpreting other people's behavior.

Follow-up

This activity is designed to help you analyze your skill at understanding other people.

When you approach someone at work, do you look at the situation from your co-worker's point of view, that is, empathetically? To successfully achieve your influence goals, you must acquire this skill.

Why assess your target?

Once you have started to consciously manage the impressions you make and have identified a clear goal, you must identify who is important in getting your goal accomplished. Every attempt at influence will begin by evaluating your target. The target may be a boss, an equal on the team, or even a junior you may want to persuade to do something which he or she does not wish to do. With all targets, you must fully understand their values, interests, and attitudes in order to successfully manage them.

Writing about the attributes of leaders, John Gardner notes that:

"Leaders must understand the various constituencies with whom they work. ... At the heart of skill in dealing with people is social perceptiveness – the ability to appraise accurately the readiness or resistance of followers ... to make the most of the motives that are there, and to understand the sensitivities."[1]

The legendary Speaker of the House, Tip O'Neill, is a classic example of a leader who understood these "various constituencies:"

"Part of the reason for O'Neill's success is his understanding of human weakness. In a system built on mutual dependence, those with no insight into the nature of frailty never get very far .... As he likes to say, you put the people together, job by job, favor by favor, and you get a program, a bill, a policy."[2]

The corporate heads of CBS, Frank Stanton and William Paley, demonstrate the importance of assessing and managing your target.[3] Stanton wanted operational control of CBS while Paley wanted to maintain ultimate authority. The two men had little in common. In addition, Paley was a hire-and-fire merchant who often sacked people without warning. To ensure survival, Stanton had to understand Paley and to have a coping strategy. His solution was to avoid threatening or challenging Paley in public, in order to maintain Paley's feelings of being the boss:

> "Although Stanton was only seven years younger than Paley, the two men assumed a father–son manner marked by Stanton's unwavering filial respect ... in the presence of their subordinates .... In meetings, Stanton submerged his ego, never taking issue with Paley. As he grew more experienced, he learned to reflect an opposing viewpoint by attributing it to others .... When Stanton expressed his own opinion, it was to agree with the boss."[4]

RECENT FINDINGS

Research[5] confirms that accurate interpretation of other people's behavior is important – a survey of 150 US and UK executives found that the "ability to understand people" was rated the most important of 16 management skills by the US executives and as second most important by their UK counterparts.[5]

Other research found that the more perceptive a leader was of his or her subordinates' strengths and weaknesses, the more successful the leader proved to be.[6] For example, the success of Ronald Reagan's first term as President was often held to stem from his ability to create and manage a close circle of complementary advisors – a man of perhaps limited technical ability, the "Great Communicator" was nonetheless a very perceptive leader.

Assessing others is usually a subconscious process which anyone in business goes through several times a day. We are always trying to work out other people's inner states and qualities, their behavior, how they will react to a given proposal, whether they share the same sense of humor, and so on.

This process matters because what the others think, feel and say will determine to a large extent how we respond – whether we smile, what topics of conversation we will touch upon, how far we will push a proposal.

The objective of this chapter is to develop this *unconscious* assessment of others into a *conscious* process; at the same time, the chapter will teach the skills associated with understanding other people and interpreting their behavior.

Learning to perceive

The way in which we interpret other people is a largely unconscious and instantaneous process. The key to improving your skills in person-perception is to become fully aware of this process.

Being aware of the perception process and of the various rules guiding your behavior and your perception of others, will help to avoid some of the pitfalls. These errors include overlooking individual differences in people, interpreting situations only from your own frame of reference, assuming similarity, and selecting out or distorting new information which does not fit your scheme of things.

The five-stage person-perception process

How does the process of person interpretation work? Psychologists say that there are five key steps to successfully understanding other people and interpreting their behavior – (1): look for cues; (2): decide what the cues mean; (3): develop behavioral stereotypes; (4): determine what triggered the behavior; (5): make a judgment.

> There are five key steps to successfully understanding other people and interpreting their behavior.

■ Step 1: Look for cues

The first step is to look for cues, because cues convey or express meaning about a person's likely behavior. For example, "he had a limp handshake" is much more than a comment on poor muscle tone in the hands.

In addition, cues may express meaning either unintentionally

or intentionally. The limp handshake could signal either unfriend-
liness (intentional) or a weak personality (unintentional). Similarly, someone could smile at you either intentionally to
demonstrate warmth, or unintentionally because he or she found
your appearance amusing – and was simply unable to keep a
straight face.

A real-life example to illustrate this process might be Lord
King, chairman of British Airways, meeting Richard Branson. He
noted that Branson was soft-spoken, sported a beard and wore
woollen sweaters.

■ Step 2: What do the cues mean?

The next step is to assemble the various cues as you would a
jigsaw puzzle, in order to build up a picture of what a person's
behavior toward you might be.

So we might use the cues that Sue was fat, had red hair and
wore large, red-rimmed glasses to infer that she was a rather jolly
extrovert. Similarly, commonly held identification rules might
lead us to perceive businessmen with beards as psychologically
stronger then clean-shaven executives.

This process means that we often make big generalizations
about the people we meet, such as are they happy or sad, lazy or
committed, confident or insecure. Real life is not always so clear
cut – most people fall between the two extremes.

So we must be careful not to draw general impressions of a
person on the basis of a single characteristic, such as intelligence,
sociability, or appearance. If we do, we run the risk of creating a
halo or horns effect. The halo effect means that should we perceive a single characteristic in a person's behavior as particularly
favorable, then we are likely to make the general observation that
the rest of that individual's behavior is equally favorable. The
converse is equally true – this is the horns effect.

In our earlier example, Lord King took the cues to mean that
Branson was nonthreatening.

■ Step 3: Develop behavioral stereotypes

The next step is to develop stereotypes based on the qualities which we imply from the cues.

We tend to label people with traits or qualities which typically belong to what psychologists call the "reference group" to which they belong. For example, all salesmen are aggressive loud mouths; all accountants are quiet introverts. But by using stereotypes, you can build up a false picture of the person which ignores the reality. In Lord King's mind, serious businessmen wore suits. Branson did not. Branson was, therefore, not a serious businessman.

Tiny Rowland, to take another example, fully understood how to exploit to his advantage the power of stereotyping on the basis of a few attributes. Accordingly he hid his background as a German-born immigrant by presenting himself as the ideal Englishman who could be implicitly trusted to conform to the establishment's code: "Dressed in his immaculate suits, monogrammed silk shirts and highly polished shoes, Rowland gave the impression of the quintessential, manicured, perfectly accented Englishman."[7]

Stereotypes are important in helping us to deal with the enormous amount of people we encounter in our everyday lives. We simply do not have the time it takes to get to know them properly. We are, therefore, obliged to use shortcuts based on past experience.

You must be careful not to assume that any one factor determines a person: people are multifaceted. You may expect an accountant to be a numbers-driven "bean-counter," only to discover that he perceives himself to be an intuitive, fully rounded businessman with strong strategic skills.

For almost every stereotype there is an exception. So the initial benefit that stereotypes may provide in making judgments must be developed by the subsequent collection of more information about your influence target.

Academic studies found that managers who were ranked the "most internationally effective" by their colleagues altered their stereotypes to fit the actual people involved, whereas managers ranked as "least internationally effective" continued to maintain their stereotypes even in the face of contradictory evidence.[8]

■ Step 4: What triggered the behavior?

A parallel process to those discussed so far is deciding whether a person's action is due to his own character (i.e. internal factors), or due to the power of the situation in which that person finds himself. Psychologists call this process "attribution theory."[9,10]

> We tend to have poor or non-existent relationships with those people to whom we attribute negative intentions.... Always remember that when you find yourself assigning negative attributes to others, situational or external factors may be the true cause of their behavior.

We underestimate the extent to which external factors influence others' behavior; conversely, we overestimate the extent to which internal and personal factors influence their behavior. For example, a customer might cancel a meeting at short notice. You could attribute this to a breakdown in the trading relationship, whereas in fact the true cause is that the customer is being visited by the chairman of his ultimate holding company.

This negative attribution cycle presents major problems for influencing successfully because it interferes with our ability to understand the potential target's world, that is, what his needs, wants, and concerns are.

We also tend to have poor or non-existent relationships with those people to whom we attribute negative intentions. We distance ourselves from them, sometimes going so far as to avoid them. This negative attribution cycle can easily develop if you overassume intentionality – that is, overassume to what extent people are acting intentionally.

Always remember that when you find yourself assigning negative attributes to others, situational or external factors may be the true cause of their behavior.

■ Step 5: Make a judgment

In parallel with the previous processes, we make moral judgments about people: are they good or bad, right or wrong?

When emotions are running high, the tendency to introduce a moral perspective is very strong. But this moral element from your side will often prevent you from seeing the situation from the other's point of view. This can lead to mistakes: what to you may seem to be an outright, morally wrong lie, may be a simple mistake within the other's framework.

It is all too easy to unconsciously judge people from our own personal perspective, based on our own personal beliefs, values, and attitudes. This personal perspective can blind us to the reality of our influence target. We will fail to take into account individual variations in people's behavior; we will systematically make biassed judgments; and we will become locked into, and unwilling to review, our thinking about an individual even in the face of contradictory evidence.

To influence effectively, we need to fully understand our influence targets and to avoid the types of interpretation errors which are discussed below.

Perceptual interpretation errors

■ Individual differences in people's behavior

When we make judgments about other people's behavior, we tend to judge from our own point of view and we see what we want to see.[11] We ignore or screen out the differences in values, motives, and aspirations between us and others. This is perfectly natural. Understanding behavior from the other person's point of view can often be emotionally painful, because we may have to reexamine dearly held beliefs, values, and aspirations upon which our self-esteem rests. Refusing to acknowledge the existence of these perfectly valid differences might offer us protection from this difficult process of reassessment, but it can also be very dangerous.

Tiny Rowland is a case in point. His ultimate downfall was caused by his inability to accurately read the values, motives, and aspirations of Dieter Bock, a 53-year-old German tax expert turned property developer, and chief executive of the Adventa group.[12] By 1992, Lonrho's debts were around £950 million. Rowland had turned 75, and although he realized that the solution to Lonrho's problem lay in Germany, eastern Europe and Russia, he was simply too old to withstand the appalling climate and interminable bureaucracy of Russia to establish Lonrho's claim. His solution was to find an investor who could be persuaded that Lonrho was undervalued and that it would rebound when the recession ended. In addition, this ideal investor would know nothing of the business and thus would be utterly reliant upon Rowland to continue managing the company. Through friends in Germany, a nominee emerged, Dieter Bock:

> "Bock's quiet personality positively disarmed Rowland. The German pleaded that he had been tracking Lonrho for the past five years and was impressed by its undervalued assets. His wife was disenchanted by life in Germany, Bock continued, and wanted to educate her children in Britain. He offered Rowland a seemingly unmenacing partnership."[13]

Rowland thought that through Bock he would retain control of the business without any financial risk. Bock would invest his funds in Lonrho, and when the time was right, Bock would become dispensable. Rowland failed to decipher Bock's motives and aspirations clearly, however. He only saw him for what Bock would do for him, not for what Bock might want for himself. Rowland completely underestimated Bock's business acumen, aggression, and determination. It took only until the end of 1994 for Bock to successfully complete his dismantling of Rowland's empire.

Similarly in our case study, Laura failed to interpret correctly the values, motives, and aspirations of James. Laura wrongly assumed that James's naval background would automatically mean that he was a results-oriented businessman with a rational perspective; she also assumed that James's age meant that he was winding down and would want to take on the role of a fatherly mentor figure. By seeing only what she wanted to see, namely the opportunity to become the managing director, Laura ignored the evidence before her very eyes.

Differences in social class, occupation, culture, and education add to the difficulty of judging people clearly. The world of the navy was alien to Laura, so she was forced to use stereotypes to make judgments about James – a Royal Navy commander means a results-driven leader. By the same token, James's naval background made it difficult for him to relate to the more participative styles of management expected of him by Laura.

Laura and James struggled to connect within a single national culture. Imagine how the difficulties are magnified by the increasingly global marketplace of the 1990s. The multiplicity of different cultural environments in which business executives have to succeed across the world demands that they understand the differing styles and ways of behaving. Imagine a Swiss executive to whom punctuality is culturally important calling a meeting to which two Mediterranean business colleagues arrive one hour late. The latecomers do not think to apologize – in their culture, their behavior was perfectly acceptable.

Our vision can become very blurred when the project or person with whom we are dealing is very important to us. Think of the times when you have been sitting at the end of the phone waiting for news of a job interview. Your anxiety and your evaluation of people and circumstances will tend to make massive pendulum swings from extremely positive to extremely negative. And when the phone finally rings and you learn that you have landed the job, your mind immediately focuses exclusively on the positive elements of your interview performance and on the job itself.

In other words, high involvement in either people or projects can lead us to distort the messages or cues in a given situation – we hear what we want to hear. Tiny Rowland was so bound up with his quest for a financial savior, for example, that he ignored the evidence which in other circumstances would have caused him to be more cautious of Bock and his motives:

> "... to secure his signature, Bock set down unforeseen conditions. His investment was provisional upon Rowland's agreement, over a pre-scribed period, to sell his own fourteen percent stake. For the man who constantly boasted, 'I have never sold a Lonrho share,' Bock's demand should have been resistible, but apparently Rowland found little difficulty in succumbing. If he was not prepared to invest his own fortune to support Lonrho, the pressure from the banks to repay the unsecured debts allowed little alternative. The consolation for Rowland was that Bock, without the Chief Executive, could not understand or manage Lonrho. Retaining control and enjoying the fun without any financial risk was the rationale behind Rowland's 'milestone' decision to sell his shares to another investor and ensure sufficient money for himself and his family in the future."[14]

Likewise in our case study, when Laura demonstrated to James that the product range whose launch he had personally master-minded was a commercial disaster, he was unable to accept the truth of the information presented. Instead, James distorted the information received and portrayed Laura as the problem (cerebral, out-of-touch marketing director), simply because of his high degree of involvement in the original decision to launch the new product range.

> **High involvement in either people or projects can lead us to distort the messages or cues in a given situation – we hear what we want to hear.**

■ Assuming similarity

We all tend to attribute to others those characteristics that we believe we possess ourselves. It is obviously easier to judge people if we assume they are similar to us. For instance, if you want chal-lenges and responsibility in your job, you assume that others want the same.

This tendency of "projection" can distort your perception of others. American researchers worked with groups of managers from 14 different countries. They invited each manager to describe the work and life goals of a colleague from another country. In every case, the managers assumed that their foreign colleagues were more like themselves than they actually were.[15]

What underpins the projection of similarity is a subconscious belief that there is only one way to be and to see the world: your way. This leads you to view other people in reference to yourself and to your way of viewing the world. Machiavellian managers, for example, will tend to assume that other people are just as Machiavellian and, therefore, relate to them on this level. By making such assumptions, they run the risk of screening out a range of strategies which might have influenced that individual effectively.

■ The locked-in effect

How often do potential influencers find that their target's mind is closed and that they cannot find a way of reaching their target? This reluctance to accept any new information which does not conform with your current way of viewing the world is natural.[16] Consider how difficult the average voter finds it to change political party, even when he is highly dissatisfied with his current choice. Many people in this situation decide not to vote at all, in preference to taking on a new party which might not sit so comfortably with their existing beliefs and values. In addition, the faster we form our impression of people and situations, the harder it is for us to accept more accurate information at a later stage.

Margaret Thatcher's relationship with UK Cabinet minister Cecil Parkinson exemplifies this locked-in effect. Thatcher had a

> Machiavellian managers will tend to assume that others are just as Machiavellian and, therefore, relate to them on this level. By making such assumptions, they run the risk of screening out a range of strategies which might have influenced that individual effectively.

liking for good-looking men which seemed to increase if they were capable of even the slightest flirtation with her. She perceived this as mutual chemistry between two people and was highly flattered by it. She reacted instinctively either for or against people. Having made an instant and instinctive judgment on someone, she was unlikely to change her mind. Thus it was with Cecil Parkinson. When the affair between the married Parkinson and his former secretary, Sara Keays, became public knowledge and threatened a political scandal, Thatcher was reluctant to change her mind about making him foreign secretary:

> "... Cecil visited me in Downing Street and told me that he had been having an affair with his former secretary, Sara Keays. This gave me pause. But I did not immediately decide that it was an insuperable obstacle to his becoming Foreign Secretary. I was still thinking about the election. Indeed, I marvelled that with all this on his mind he had run such a magnificent campaign. ...
>
> "I wanted if possible to keep Cecil – a political ally, an able minister and a friend."[17]

All of these mistakes in interpretation can cause us to fail in understanding and predicting how the influence target will react. You may feel that you are not susceptible to the locked-in effect because you always consult with your colleagues to gather information about the influence target. Unfortunately, colleagues are not always the most useful source. The people whose opinions you most trust are quite often those who see the world most similarly to yourself. It is precisely the sharing of biases and assumptions which often makes for trusted colleague relationships. All this does is increase the comfort, but reinforce the distortion.

Use multiple indicators

To avoid breakdowns in the process of understanding your influence target, you must stand back from yourself, leave your own values and assumptions to one side, admit that your own guesses may be wrong and start to build up knowledge about the target.

You should seek out a range of indicators to understand your influence target. These multiple indicators include verbal and such nonverbal cues as posture, interpersonal distance, gesture, tone of voice, and eye contact. They also include organizational and personal factors, such as the demands of the target's job, how he is assessed and rewarded, his pressure points, career and educational background, values, and interests.[18] All these indicators can then combine to present a much more developed understanding of your target. The more you know, the better able you are to speak the target's language, match the target's style and key into what is important to him.

The next section highlights the key indicators to help you understand your target's world.

■ Nonverbal cues

One of the most basic indicators we can use to understand our influence target, particularly in the early stages of an interaction when we may have little other evidence from which to work, is the target's body language or nonverbal behavior. Research by Ekman and Friesen suggests that body language can help the potential influencer in five main ways.[19]

In the first place, body language is usually less well-controlled and manipulated by people than other verbal forms of behavior. A flushed face or sweating brow speak volumes about how your target is actually thinking and feeling.

Secondly, body language can provide important cues about how the target regards his relationship with you – this is particularly useful information in the early stages of an attempt to exercise influence, when body language can express what verbal language cannot and does not. For example, a warm handshake suggests that your target is expressing generally positive feelings toward you – it would be inappropriate for the target to explicitly articulate these sentiments.

In addition, body language provides important symbolic cues which we can use to plan and guide our interaction. For example, a simple nod can have strong symbolic overtones about how someone is thinking in a tense business meeting.

Equally important is the value of body language in providing us with important cues about how the target thinks and feels about himself: such as, strong or weak, anxious or confident.

The fifth way in which body language helps the influencer is when the influencer manages his own body language to influence the target's perception of, and reaction to, the influencer – this relates to the sixth principle of influence – emotion. When you are appraising a subordinate, you can encourage open communication by how you sit (that is, not directly opposite in a confrontational way), by maintaining good eye contact, by smiling, by keeping an open body posture, and so on.

That said, we must avoid the trap of reading cues which simply are not there – some people habitually stoop, purse their lips, and frown – as people say, "it's just their manner."

Physical appearance

Does the person you want to influence prefer the clean-cut look; the horn-rimmed, thoughtful academic type; the macho, champagne-drinking, red suspenders and shirt-sleeves type; or the slim, muscular fitness fanatic?

There are many physical stereotypes which we use to link personality characteristics to physical appearance. It is important to ensure that you interpret these as accurately as possible, because the more closely you can match your appearance to fit your target's comfort zone and particular likes, the more successful you will be.

You do not necessarily have to fundamentally change your own image. But you may need to become marginally more conservative in your dress or style, for example. This type of matching shows that you identify with your target and so helps the target to feel comfortable in working with you or in supporting you.

Some managers feel that self-presentation is unimportant relative to the substance of an issue. If that is correct, ask yourself why political image-makers such as Tim Bell and Peter Mandelson wield so much authority in British politics today. Margaret Thatcher was sensitive to the usefulness of adjusting her personal image to match the comfort zone of the British electorate: elocution lessons softened her voice to make her appear less strident; major work was done to her teeth; a hairdresser came regularly to Downing Street in the early hours so that Mrs Thatcher would always look her best for the day, leading to some unkind comparisons with the then Shirley Williams, who demonstrated perhaps less concern with her physical turnout. Former Labour Party leader, Michael Foot was always identified by the duffel coat which he wore even at a formal Remembrance Day event – a far cry from New Labour's double-breasted suits.

You should also exercise caution when evaluating the physical characteristics of your target because stereotypes based on physical characteristics are determined by culture. Japanese culture, for example, emphasizes a respect for elders, whereas American culture is more youth-oriented. Thus an older, white-haired employee might be viewed by a Japanese manager as offering valuable experience, whilst an American manager might see the same individual as being over the hill.

There are even different physical stereotypes associated with different business sectors. For example, the music business is characterized by a more casual, young look, whereas accountancy tends to favor sober navy blue suits, white shirts, conservative ties, and short hair.

Equally important are body movements, gestures, touch, facial expressions, eye contact, and interpersonal distance – all of which are important signals to watch for when interpreting your influence target. Take eye contact as an example.

Eye contact

Eye contact is particularly important in understanding and then influencing your target. Research suggests that eye contact helps to regulate the flow of communication as well as monitoring feedback, expressing emotion, and providing important cues about the nature of the relationship – friendly and warm, or withdrawn and distant.[20]

**RECENT
FINDINGS**

> A number of important cues can be picked up from the way in which we gaze at each other. A basic rule to bear in mind when you are interpreting the message behind the target's gaze is that the average length of an individual gaze is three seconds. This compares with the average duration of a mutual gaze – that is, when you both look at each other simultaneously – of about one second. The research reports that you can judge the intensity of a relationship by the length of mutual gaze – the more intense the relationship, the longer the length of mutual gaze.[21]

Gaze can also be used to interpret status and positioning in a relationship. Higher status people, for example, spend less time gazing at lower status people than vice-versa.[22]

Eye contact can also be used as a weapon to threaten the other person – people subjected to prolonged stares often interpret them as aggressive and may rapidly retreat from the situation. As Margaret Thatcher's biographer commented:

> "She does not even drop her gaze as so many women do. ... Instead, the pale blue eyes – paler and more Arctic with the passing years – stare into the other's face. Rather than look down, the eyes are much more likely to narrow, such as when a journalist friend of mine interviewed her and brought the discussion around to her retirement. He recalls: 'The eyes narrowed, the coldness of the eyes became quite terrifying and the very temperature in the room seemed to chill.'"[23]

We can use gaze to signal our desire to open a conversation. Conversely, we may withdraw eye contact when we wish to close a conversation or deny eye contact to "freeze someone out."

Touch

Touch is another important nonverbal signal for
managers, helping you to judge the degree of empathy and mutual liking in a relationship as well as the
level of mutual self-disclosure, that is, the extent to
which you are comfortable with the person.[24]

Higher status people are more likely to touch; lower status people are more likely to be touched.

Like gaze, touch can be used to define status. Traditionally the
British monarch has had a policy of no touching in public in order
to define her status. During a recent visit to Australia, the then
prime minister, Paul Keating, put his arm around the Queen in
what many defined as an act deliberately symbolizing the diminishing status of the monarchy in Australia.

Higher status people are more likely to touch; lower status
people are more likely to be touched. Perhaps Mrs Thatcher's
renowned habit of extending her arm to shuffle along the rest of
the European Union heads of state at meetings was a way of symbolizing her perceived higher status.

Remember that men and women may perceive touch differently: for women, being touched may carry sexual overtones.
Touch also means different things in different cultures. Russian
men commonly hug; Japanese people have an aversion to body
contact and prefer to bow; in France, you shake hands with
people you know each time that you meet – not quite the done
thing in Great Britain plc.

Interpersonal distance

A very important signal in understanding other people is interpersonal distance, how physically close you are to your target. In
trying to establish close empathetic relationships with your influence target, you should be aware of how the degree of interpersonal distance can signify changes in levels of intimacy and
interest on the part of your target.

Margaret Thatcher's penchant for good-looking men, particularly those in uniform, was particularly apparent: "… sometimes

in the early hours, when with people she knows, she will kick off her shoes and sit at the foot of the best-looking man in the room."[25]

RECENT FINDINGS

Everybody is familiar with the phrase – "Give me some space." The anthropologist Edward Hall has actually proposed a set of distance zones to describe various patterns of interaction.[26] For Americans, the four major zones and the distance they span are:

1. **Intimate** – physical contact to 18 inches

2. **Personal** – 18 inches to 4 feet

3. **Social** – 4 feet to 12 feet

4. **Public** – 12 feet to 25 feet

The intimate zone is acceptable in typical, close family relationships; the personal zone is right for friends and acquaintances; the social zone defines what is comfortable for business and casual social interaction; whilst the public zone refers to formal interactions, like standing in line.

There are of course wide cultural variations in the size of inter-personal distance zones. Look at people waiting in line in a London post office where many nationalities are represented and you can positively sense the discomfort when one person's public zone is much less than another's.

■ Verbal cues

Your request is most likely to succeed when it is phrased in terms with which your target is comfortable and which express values held by the target. Academics refer to this process as "framing your request in the correct currency."

It follows from this that you should seek out clues which identify your target's "currency." Analyzing your target's language is among the best ways of achieving this.

Verbal behavior – how people speak and what they say – can

convey much information about how the person operates. Words are like neon signs, they serve as markers of the underlying factors when you try to understand your target.

In the business world, for example, Richard Branson's soft, almost hesitant and shy, school-boy manner has been one of his most effective tools in influencing those around him and in giving the impression of modesty. It was written of his negotiations with American record executives that:

> "To executives more accustomed to the slick, desk-pounding, hustling and screaming school of salesmanship, Branson's gauche, school-boy manner and his abashed confessions that 'actually, I'm not sure who produced this one' proved quite appealing ..."[27]

The target's style of speech provides you with important cues about how that person operates as an individual and how we should relate to that person. Take Kelvin MacKenzie of the *Sun* newspaper – he established a specific style of relating to others using verbal assault as his standard form of speech when he became editor. A typical example concerns Mike Terry, the elderly, bespectacled features editor after just a week into the job:[28]

> "All right, are we today, Mike, eh? Woken up yet, have we, Mike? Brain working? Lights on are they, Mike, eh? Anyone at home, Mike, eh, eh? Now, come on, Mike. Tell me the truth, Mike, eh? Now don't look away, Mike. Because we're not always at home, eh, Mike? Not always in, are we, eh, eh?."[29]

Many of the journalists like Mike Terry would crumble under such bullying attacks. However, those hacks who could key into MacKenzie's language could maintain influence with him:

> "Occasionally, but only very occasionally, somebody with enough cheek put one over on him. One show biz hack, after ten minutes of rant, seized his chance as MacKenzie paused to draw breath. Giving a wink, he grinned and said quickly: 'You're going to give me a bollocking now, aren't you, Kelvin?' MacKenzie, completely disarmed,

burst out laughing and dismissed him with a delighted wave of the arm and a dismissive: 'Go on then. **** off out of here.'"[30]

The language used by our target provides important clues about how the target perceives his or her social position. This is nothing new. The word *malapropism* comes from the eighteenth-century playwright Sheridan, whose character Mrs Malaprop used language to try to position herself above her class. She had the misfortune of giving the game away by declaring that someone was "as headstrong as an *allegory* [alligator] on the banks of the Nile."

The reverse tactic can also be played. Kelvin MacKenzie realized this: his projected image of a working-class background was highly influential in securing his appointment as editor of the *Sun* and it served as his standard tool for influencing and managing his editorial staff:

"All the time he would be playing the yob, the sarff [south] London hard man. ... His comfy middle-class background had now been buried in the new image of the self-made man risen from the working classes. The whispering disinformation went round – the one O-level [exam pass], now said to be in woodwork, showed not that he was thick, but how he didn't give a toss about the system; he had been expelled from his posh school, they told each other; he'd been brought up in a council flat [public housing]; he really came from rough Peckham, not more genteel Camberwell. With his background it was obvious he was the one who understood the readers, who knew what they wanted. Middle-class pretensions were there to be trashed and rubbished."[31]

How we say things is as important as *what* we say. Pitch changes, rhythm, intensity, rapidity, and pauses all constitute "paralanguage,"[32] the physical side of language. For errant Conservative Party ministers, for example, being verbally worked-over by Margaret Thatcher became known as being "hand-bagged."

Kelvin MacKenzie was another who used paralanguage to excellent effect in influencing his staff:

"MacKenzie would start a stream of patter, speaking quietly and reasonably, but putting in the needle by continuously adding the general enquiry 'Eh, eh?' in a way which gave them no choice but to nod in agreement. 'Look at you lot, eh?' he would start, 'Useless load of *******, aren't you, eh? Right load of *******, eh, eh?.'"[33]

There are various common patterns. Rapid-fire speech may indicate excitement or anxiety. If the talker does not hold eye contact or continually looks away, this is telling the listener that he or she is not important. A low-pitched voice has a different meaning than a high-pitched voice – pleasantness, boredom, or sadness, rather than fear, surprise, or anger.

In addition, silences can have a wide variety of meanings, from use as a tactic to seek agreement through to simply serving as a pause to allow people thinking time. Silence tends to produce discomfort, which may lead one participant in a conversation to remove the discomfort by talking. It is, therefore, a highly effective pressure tactic. Silence is even more effective on the telephone, when the person you are seeking to pressure can gain no solace from nonverbal cues because you are invisible.

The factors above represent just the start to accurately diagnosing your target. To fully understand the world of your potential targets, you must discover their concerns and objectives, the nature of the job they have to do, how they are rewarded and measured, their contact base, the pressure points they face, career aspirations, personal background, their values, interests, and so on.

Discovering this information is fundamental for determining how you are going to influence your targets. Some of the information will be relatively straightforward, but as we have shown when discussing the mistakes you can make in perceiving others, you may need to reassess or spend more time gathering information before you can accurately understand your target.

> **Silence tends to produce discomfort, which may lead one participant in a conversation to remove the discomfort by talking. It is, therefore, a highly effective pressure tactic.**

We will now turn to a consideration of this other information required.

■ Factors pertaining to the organization

Understanding your target's job

To influence effectively, you must understand your influence target's job role – his tasks, responsibilities, style of working (numbers- or people-driven). How much power does he or she wield – whether in terms of calling the shots or providing a service to others?

Information such as this will suggest the correct way to frame your attempt to exercise influence – in terms of the correct style to use, what buttons there are to be pushed. In the case study, for example, Laura might have approached the issue of the ill-fated product launch and its subsequent turnaround quite differently had she fully appreciated that a major feature of James's job was to consistently present himself to his board at global headquarters in the best possible light.

Sir Bernard Ingham certainly realized what was important to Margaret Thatcher when she became prime minister:

> "Margaret Thatcher was seeking to blaze her new economic trail in the face of an unexpected massive hike in the price of oil that was plunging the world into recession. Many of her own Conservative back-benchers thought she would be ditched before the next General Election. ... What Bernard Ingham saw was a threatened but very determined woman with vision. ... He picked up her vision and, on her behalf, he ran with it."[34]

How is your target's performance assessed and rewarded?

There is an old management truism that what gets done is what is *inspected*, not what is *expected*. Departmental performance indicators subject to inspection might include overtime, delivery performance, levels of stockholding, market share, product profitability, overdue accounts, and so on.

People are often assessed and rewarded on the basis of their performance against indicators specific to their function. The goals of one department will sometimes conflict with those of others. To develop business with a key customer targeted for growth and so increase market share, for example, a marketing manager may accept a loss-making order which can only be supplied in time by incurring overtime. This causes immediate conflict with production and finance.

Step four in the process of person-perception alerted you to the fact that we all too often attribute people's behavior to factors peculiar to them as individuals (internal factors), rather than to the situation in which they find themselves. This can cause major errors of judgment, which inhibit our ability to influence effectively. In the example above of the marketing manager, he or she may perceive that his or her praiseworthy efforts are being deliberately thwarted by the negative obstruction of production and finance. The marketer may not realize that the people in production and finance are merely doing their jobs and performing consistently with the measures against which they are rewarded.

The target's pressure points

You need to be aware of the target's pressure points. Your target will inevitably depend on a whole web of third parties to achieve his objectives – these third parties will include people inside the company (such as the sales force, production, and the unions), people inside the group holding company (such as the chief executive or group personnel director), as well as people outside the company (such as bankers, analysts, competitors, and suppliers).

Each of these third parties will have a different claim on, and exert a different pressure over, your target. To influence successfully, you need to understand where your target's existing pressure points are so that you can frame your attempt appropriately.

Another way to look at it is to ask yourself what keeps your influence target awake at night. You will never get what you want from your target if you cannot pinpoint his anxiety zone – whether it is long-term competition from the Pacific Rim, the impact of new technology, or the failure of a recent product launch.

You should also consider how your target's third party contacts may have a bearing on you. For example, one of the factors which was influential in Laura's relationship with James was the latter's potential to block any communication between Laura and the American headquarters. This meant that should Laura ever have needed to make direct contact with headquarters, the people there would already have been influenced by the distorted image of her given by James.

In summary, an awareness of the contacts and pressures which your influence target experiences gives you a good indication of which buttons to push and, just as importantly, which to avoid.

> You will never get what you want from your target if you cannot pinpoint his anxiety zone – whether it is long-term competition from the Pacific Rim, the impact of new technology, or the failure of a recent product launch.

■ Personal factors

Career aspirations and personal background

You need to understand where your influence target has come from and where he or she is headed. Allan Cohen and David Bradford suggest a number of useful pointers on this.[35]

If you have encountered your target before, it is likely that you will already have this information. Gaining information on people with whom you have had little contact at best, or bad dealings at worst, is more difficult.

The target's career aspirations will significantly shape his attitude to people, situations, and risk. A manager who has suffered three redundancies in as many years may well have a quite different attitude to risk when compared to a sure-footed, fast-track manager who is anxious to make his or her mark. Indeed, one of the recent criticisms of marketing brand managers is that they are biassed toward initiating short-term, high-profile marketing programs which generate publicity for them as individuals in the trade press, without necessarily staying long enough in the job to see through the full effects – good or bad – of their efforts.

Remember the constant dangers of stereotyping. After all, consider how wrong Laura's assessment of James was – nothing could have been further from the truth than the stereotype of the father figure gracefully winding down to retirement.

Where did your target study, and to what level? In some organizations, managers without a business qualification will see it as their sacred duty to knock MBAs and their equivalents off their pedestal.

Where did he or she work before? What did he or she do and how? It is a reasonable assumption that a marketing director promoted to managing director of a previously production-led company will alter the strategic emphasis of his or her new company. Likewise, company "doctors" tend to use the same prescriptions in the different companies whose health they are sent to restore – either by replacing labor with capital or by restructuring into smaller, strategic business units. Similarly, though on a more general level, Tom Peters highlighted the fact that knowledge of other people's career histories brings insight into the "recipes" which brought them success in their previous jobs and which they will doubtless seek to use again in their new ones.

Managers who have operated all their lives in a single industry may well view issues and problems from a different perspective from managers who have worked in a variety of industries and can cross-fertilize ideas.

What is the target's previous style of working – does he slowly build up a picture of the situation and develop consensus around his proposed solutions, or is his first action to fire some of the managers in order to set the tone, and then determine what to do next?

What bad experiences has your target suffered in the past – strategic issues which went wrong, bosses or subordinates with whom there was conflict? Your target will inevitably wish to avoid recurrence of such situations – insider knowledge on your behalf gives you an edge into how he will probably react to specific proposals or recommendations which touch a similar nerve.

Values

We have already discussed how your own personal values affect the personal style you tend to use. By the same token, your target is influenced by his or her values. This means that you must discover what these values are.

Does your target favor soft or strong management styles? Does he categorize people according to theory X or theory Y: inevitably lazy and nonmotivated (theory X), or inherently good, self-motivated and self-managing (theory Y)? Does your target believe that the organization comprises equal partners, "them and us," or "officers and the ranks"?

If your influence target is a man, how does he regard women – as equals, or as things to focus on at the office Christmas party? How does a female boss view other aspiring female colleagues – Margaret Thatcher was notorious for never having another woman in her Cabinet: what should this tell us about her attitudes and values as far as other female executives were concerned?

Similarly, the person who thinks that anything is negotiable will react entirely differently from someone who sticks to a few tightly held views.

Interests

A great deal of evidence can be gleaned about the interests and motivation of the individual by just observing his or her personal office space. Is the gym or squash kit left next to the desk, are

training certificates plastered over the walls, do family photographs have pride of place over sales graphs? All these types of
personal cues can provide opportunities to build relationships
and find common ground with your influence target. Laura, for
example, made the constant mistake of ignoring James's interests
in everything nautical.

All of the factors discussed in this chapter can provide clues to
what might be important to your potential target, and to how you
should frame your influence goal. The more information you can
gather about the target's organizational situation, personality, and
personal situation, the more accurate your perception of that
person will be. The more accurate your perception, the better
equipped you will be to work on those behaviors, values, attitudes, and ideas that your target can accept, tolerate, and manage.
You will also be better prepared to manage the interaction process
itself so that both parties feel comfortable.

You do not need to have every detail in the world about your
target – a few key relevant facts will at least point you in the right
direction. The greater your knowledge, however, the wider the
range of influence tactics open to you and the smaller the risk of
making errors of perception based on ignorance.

CHAPTER SUMMARY

- This chapter has focussed on the need to identify who is important in getting your goal accomplished, and on correctly interpreting the kind of behavior, values, attitudes, and ideas which your influence target can accept. This puts you firmly in control of the influence process.

- We have stressed the need to consciously manage the way in which you perceive people so that you do not fall into the routine errors of interpretation. An important aspect of this conscious perception management is to draw upon multiple indicators (such as verbal and nonverbal cues, organizational factors, and personal issues), as well as to avoid making so-called, common-sense judgments which may mislead.

CONCEPT QUIZ

Do you understand how to interpret people's behavior effectively and increase your influence power?

1. The mark of good managers is the speed with which they can make accurate assessments of other people. *True or false?*

2. First impressions are the most accurate impressions. *True or false?*

3. We are more inclined to attribute other people's behavior to the situations in which they find themselves, than to their personalities. *True or false?*

4. Observing someone's body language is a waste of time. *True or false?*

5. Language is a very powerful way to draw clues about someone's attitudes and motives. *True or false?*

6. It is a waste of management time getting to know people's interests, worries, and values. *True or false?*

7. Reviewing stereotypes on the basis of subsequent information is a waste of time. *True or false?*

8. The way you dress at work is important in determining your success in influencing others. *True or false?*

9. Managers are pretty much the same whatever country you visit. *True or false?*

10. Matching your general behavioral style to fit the comfort zone of your target is a waste of time. *True or false?*

Answers

1(T), 2(F), 3(F), 4(F), 5(T), 6(F), 7(F), 8(T), 9(F), 10(F).

LAURA OPENS HER EYES

Laura realized from her experience to date in her new company that she was failing to judge her colleagues correctly. She acknowledged that she had assessed James solely from her own point of view, and so had failed to reach him effectively.

Laura was determined not to make the same mistake again. Accordingly, she saw the appointment in the States of Mike Stamper to the post of associate director, group market research, as an opportunity to improve her skills at evaluating people.

Given that Mike was shortly going to spend six months' secondment in the UK division, she felt that any information she could glean in advance when she herself was in the States would surely come in useful.

Following their first meeting at group headquarters, the Laura of old would have characterized Stamper as a rational, results-driven individual like herself. Once bitten, twice shy, however. The new Laura had decided to take an almost clinical interest in developing a dossier of key information about the new associate director.

During a break at a later market research ideas workshop, Laura complimented Mike on his expensive and rather flamboyant tie. Flattered, Mike boasted that it was a present from a previous girlfriend and that his current wife passionately disliked him wearing it. From this brief exchange, Laura added vanity to the dossier on Mike.

Laura also heard on the grapevine that Mike treated his subordinates as if he were an old-fashioned captain of industry, and used a very autocratic, "whips and chains" management style. Laura concluded that Mike's need for recognition of his status was very high.

Laura also noticed that, during the absence of any of the members of the main board, Mike liked to use their offices to hold meetings, claiming that their air conditioning was more effective than his. Even Laura was able to recognize that Mike saw himself as the heir apparent to the main board marketing director.

Laura decided to capitalize on these findings during Mike's secondment to the UK operation. Once back in the UK, Laura made elaborate preparations for Mike's arrival, reserving Mike's parking space with a personalized sign, flooding the marketing department with photographs of their VIP visitor so that Mike would be instantly recognized, and arranging an elaborate buffet lunch commensurate with the status of an associate director. Over lunch, Laura even went so far as to make innu-endoes about Mike's elevation to the main board. The key market research issues facing the UK operation were not touched upon.

Mike sat in on James's next team meeting. Laura was pleased to see that when James referred one of her more controversial market research proposals to Mike for his approval, Mike declared without hesitation that the proposal was absolutely rock-solid and should be actioned immediately, if not sooner.

Review question

1. What did Laura do right?

SUMMARY CHECKLIST

❏ Identify your influence targets.

❏ Make the assessment of your target a conscious process.

❏ Watch and listen for cues.

❏ Identify what the cues infer about the target's moods, attitudes, or intentions – in other words, about his or her attributes.

❏ Link these attributes with other attributes.

❏ Consider whether the target's behavior is driven by personality characteristics or situational factors.

❏ Make a judgment.

❏ Build up a file of information about your target.

❏ Beware of ignoring individual differences, stereotyping, assuming similarity, and attributing everything to personality factors.

ACTION CHECKLIST

1. Do not assume people will behave consistently in different situations and do not overlook the situational causes of their behavior.

_____

_____

2. Do not try too hard to construct a consistent picture of others by thinking that all good things go together; be willing to recognize that they may be both intelligent and lazy, neurotic and generous.

_____

_____

3. Do not be influenced too much by first impressions, in particular by physical appearance and accent, and do not apply the corresponding stereotypes. .

_____

_____

4. Do not make automatically positive evaluations of, and give favorable ratings to, people from the same town, school, or social class as yourself.

_____

_____

5. Do not be influenced too much by other people's negative points, and not enough by their positive features.

_____

_____

6. Do not constantly use stereotypes to evaluate people.

_____

_____

7. Make a conscious effort to pay adequate attention to, and demonstrate sufficient interest in, other people.

_____

_____

8. Practice empathetic behavior – that is, try to view the world as your target sees it.

_____

_____

9. Be consciously aware of the judgments you are making and the cues on which you are basing them.

_____

_____

10. Always ask yourself why you are making the judgments you are of your target.

_____

_____

chapter
five

STEP THREE – DIAGNOSE THE SYSTEM

This chapter focuses on the relationship between understanding the hidden system of the organization and successful use of influence.

The hidden system is seen as a stronger determinant of what types of influencing behavior are acceptable in the organization than the "proper" channels of authority, particularly in flat interdependent organizations.

The chapter examines organizational culture and organizational networks as prime components of this hidden system. It argues that it is culture which provides information on the kinds of behavior the organization is willing to accept, and that it is through networking that the manager actively uses this information to work the system.

Analyzing the hidden system is a key step toward success in influencing others.

SELF–ASSESSMENT EXERCISE

Evaluating your awareness of the hidden system

A good way to start assessing your personal understanding of the hidden system of the organization is to answer the following short quiz. It is designed to help you understand what the informal system is all about and how it affects the behavior you should adopt in order to successfully get things done in organizations.

Answer "yes" or "no" depending on which answer best suits your current situation.

1. Do you feel that you generally know what the values of your organization are, what is important in the company, and which projects matter? *Yes or no?*

2. Do you understand who gets ahead in your organization and why? *Yes or no?*

3. Do you think about how long people stay in jobs, particularly middle managers? *Yes or no?*

4. Do you think about the difference between the formally stated purpose of meetings, and the reality of what is actually said? *Yes or no?*

5. Do you think about the real significance underlying the stories and anecdotes which circulate around the organization? *Yes or no?*

6. Do you feel that you are generally in the know about what is going on in your organization? *Yes or no?*

7. Have you maintained contact with other groups, departments, and people as you have moved around or up the organization? *Yes or no?*

8. Do you prefer to deal with people face-to-face to discuss problems? *Yes or no?*

9. Do you share information with your sources and contacts? *Yes or no?*

10. Do you know people in other departments, such as secretaries, who can give you access to information which otherwise may not come your way? *Yes or no?*

11. Do you maintain external contacts with other professional groups, such as lawyers, accountants, advertising agencies? *Yes or no?*

12. Do you ever key into suppliers for information? *Yes or no?*

13. Do you ever attend outside conferences, trade and professional association activities, on either a formal or social basis? *Yes or no?*

14. Do you have a network of contacts among your peers in other organizations? *Yes or no?*

15. Do you have any contacts across the organization who can circulate information on your behalf? *Yes or no?*

Follow-up

To find out your score, simply circle the number of each question to which you have answered "yes."

If you answered "yes" to ten or more questions, you have a good understanding of the hidden system of the organization, of how its culture and networks operate. You are probably quite successful at exercising influence, although there is still room for improvement.

If your score was five or less, you have room for substantial improvement because you are not switched into the hidden system. It is also highly likely that you exert very limited influence within your organization.

Why the hidden system?

People often talk of doing things through the "proper channels" – this statement recognizes the fact that every organization has not only its formal "correct" structure, but also an informal, shadow structure.

Only naive managers assume that the sole way to use influence is through the formal channels. Exclusive reliance on formal channels will cause you to lose out to people who know how to use the informal system as well. Tom Peters suggests that everyone in the new world of work should develop networking skills for use throughout the organization.[1] In his study of successful general managers, John Kotter reports that the managers had literally hundreds, and sometimes even thousands, of individuals in their networks.[2]

It is essential to learn how the informal system of your organization works, and to become part of it. If you are excluded from this nonformal system, you will either be ignored or become a source of contempt and derision – in either case, your influence will be severely limited. You will be regarded as an "isolate" within the organization, somebody who works alone with limited access to information and correspondingly little power to exchange information.[3]

As we argued in chapter one, business schools are perhaps producing Masters of Business Administration rather than Masters of Business. Such rational administrators tend to be committed disciples of the formal systems of human resource management, with all its panoply of job descriptions, appraisals, disciplinary procedures, and so on.

This chapter goes a step further, however, by arguing that successful modern management very often involves bypassing these formal systems in order to get things done. This means working through and with people, in other words, through the culture of the organization. This allows you to tap into the "soft side" of organizational life to mobilize people.

As stated in chapter four: *Identify your Target*, people are not the automata which rational management would have us sometimes believe they are. Instead, emotions and feelings can and do have a powerful impact on the way they think, behave, and respond to what we are trying to achieve. If you can move away from the formal systems and procedures, and tap into individuals' emotions, feelings, and behavior at the informal level, then you have a very powerful and influential basis for achieving your objectives.

Jack Welch, CEO of GE, harnessed the power of emotions and symbols to great effect when he was rising through the managerial ranks.[4] Faced with the problem of attacking the company's high cost base, he could have followed a rational route by calling in consultants, assigning his best managers to the project, or seting up project teams. He did none of these. Instead, he installed a hotline telephone in his office dedicated to taking calls from his purchasing staff. Whenever the purchasing people negotiated a price discount from a supplier, they would ring Welch with the news. Welch made it an article of faith to take the call, no matter what he was doing, enthuse the successful buyer and then follow up with a congratulatory note. This use of the informal system not only made heroes of the buyers – it made a hero of Welch himself.

GE considers the informal system to be so important that it has a program in place to allow senior managers to act as mentors to their juniors about their careers, which includes specific advice on how to beat the formal system.[5]

The world of business is changing so dramatically, with downsizing, multifunctional teams, external alliances, partnerships and business globalization (all making for much flatter organizations), that there are much fewer formal systems through which to work and exercise influence.

The coming of age of skillful manipulation of the informal system is highlighted by Rosabeth Moss Kanter of the

> If you can move away from the formal systems and procedures and tap into individuals' emotions, feelings, and behavior at the informal level, then you have a very powerful and influential basis for achieving your objectives.

Harvard Business School who argues that these flatter organizations call for a "new kind of business hero" who must learn to
operate without the might of the hierarchy behind him or her.[6] As
she says, for these new heroes "the crutch of authority must be
thrown away and replaced by their own personal ability to make
relationships, use influence, and work with others to achieve
results."[7]

At the core of this informal system are organizational culture
and human networks. So inspired is GE's Jack Welch by the
power of culture and networking as the most productive ways to
get things done that he is attempting to transform GE into a network organization, a company without boundaries where "we
knock down the walls that separate us from each other on the
inside and from our key constituencies on the outside."[8]

So let us now turn to a detailed consideration of organizational
culture and then networking.

Influence and culture

The new flat interdependent structures and systems of companies
are held together by culture. And if we are to be successful in
exerting influence, we must understand the organization's culture.

DEFINITION

**There are many different definitions of organizational culture.
Andrew Pettigrew, for example, defines it as "the behavior, actions
and values that people in an enterprise are expected to follow."[9]
Similarly, Andrew Kakabadse portrays it "as the way people in different (or sometimes similar) work organizations view the world,
their life and the way they go about their work."[10]**

Whatever definition we accept, it is clear that culture represents
an effective control mechanism in regulating the type of behavior
we can display at work. As Charles Handy, the leading London
Business School Professor and expert on organizations, argues:

"In organizations, there are deep-set beliefs about the way work
should be organised, the way authority should be exercised, people

rewarded, people controlled. What are the degrees of formalization required? How much planning and how far ahead? What combination of obedience and initiative is looked for in subordinates? Do work hours matter, or dress, or personal eccentricities? What about expense accounts, and secretaries, stock options and incentives? Do committees control, or individuals? Are there rules and procedures or only results? These are all parts of the culture of an organisation."[11]

Terrence Deal and Allen Kennedy, two of the most influential writers on culture, adopt a similar line:

"People who want to get ahead within their own companies also need to understand – at least intuitively – what makes their culture tick. ... Managers must understand very clearly how the culture works if they want to accomplish what they set out to do."[12]

By establishing constraints on what people can and cannot do, organizational culture defines what kinds of influencing behavior are acceptable in the organization. Culture conveys to the manager what is appropriate behavior. Consider, for example, the following values:

- Never leave the office before your boss.
- Keep your head down if you want to survive.
- Look busy, even if you are not.
- Before you make a decision, try it out on your boss so that he or she is never taken by surprise.
- Always refer to the chairman by his title, never by name.
- To get to the top, you must play with the team.
- It is results that count, not how you achieve them.

All of the statements above indicate to the manager what is considered to be appropriate behavior. Greeting the chairman by his title, rather than by name, for example, suggests that the company puts a high value on hierarchy, status, and tradition.

You will not find these values expressed in the induction handbook. Indeed, it may be rare to hear them spoken. But these values exist in action, and the successful influencer must identify what they are.

Culture gives the influential manager a particularly powerful insight into the many sources of information which are key to achieving objectives successfully. The stories and myths of past heroes which are passed around in the organization may be significant indicators of how your target may react to a proposal, how the company's social system operates, and what is valued and why.

These sets of values, norms, and beliefs can be so strong that they transform an organization into what Handy terms a "cohesive tribe with distinctly clannish feelings."[13] These tribal values are often reinforced by an organization's private language, its catch-phrases, and the rituals it enacts.

The Tandem Corporation, one of Silicon Valley's most highly publicized companies, typifies this tribalistic culture, with Friday afternoon "beer busts" which are attended by all staff, its golf course, swimming pool, and company-wide celebrations staged on important holidays.[14]

The Walt Disney Company Parks Operation exploits its tribal culture to ensure consistency of behavior and thus consistency of the "Disney look."[15] Emphasis is placed on employing people who conform to Disney's specific standards of appearance – complexion, height, straightness and color of teeth, and so on. Recruits fresh from high school are socialized on the job into their new identities. Employees become ever-smiling "cast members"; when they work, they are "on-stage"; visitors are "guests"; rides are "attractions." To promote further behavioral consistency, the company encourages employees to spend time off work together by providing sports leagues and social events. There is no such thing as a free lunch or picnic, however: the benefit for Disney is that the risk of employees being contaminated by non-Disney values outside work is reduced.

Delta Airlines promotes a similarly strong adherence to the core company value of the "family" sticking together through thick and thin. In the industry bloodletting of the early 1980s, Delta avoided staff lay-offs by managing the expectations of its shareholders. The staff loyalty thereby engendered was later reciprocated by sacrifices on behalf of the staff for the greater good – the Delta "war stories" tell of management taking pay cuts during lean times and pilots voluntarily working fewer hours per week to keep junior employees in work.[16]

Even within a single organization, there can be different cultures: varying points of view may well exist between those working in sales, marketing, research, and administration. The accountant may prize accuracy and maintenance of the status quo, whereas the marketer may value innovation and risktaking, for example. This means that the influential manager must identify and manage these differences when a particular goal cuts across a number of different departments, divisions, or functions.

Whatever the complexity, the influential manager must be aware that:

> "In the dispersed, helter-skelter world of the radically decentralized atomized organisation. ... the role that culture plays will be even more critical than it is in today's corporate world. ... The winners in the business world of tomorrow will be the heroes who can forge the values and beliefs, the rituals and ceremonies, and a cultural network of storytellers and priests that can keep working productively in semi-autonomous units that identify with a corporate whole".[17]

Let us now look more closely at organizational cultures and consider the types of behavior which would be appropriate and thus effective in different contexts.

> Even within a single organization, there can be different cultures: varying points of view may well exist between those working in sales, marketing, research, and administration. ... This means that the influential manager must identify and manage these differences when a particular goal cuts across a number of different departments, divisions, or functions.

Types of culture

Although many models have been formulated to describe organizational culture, one of the most comprehensive and widely known is that of Dr Roger Harrison, who identifies four basic organizational cultures: power, role, task, and person.[18]

■ Power culture

DEFINITION

A power culture is strong, tough, abrasive, competitive, and challenging. Such a culture depends on strong leadership from the center – either a central power figure or a small group – which controls and manipulates all activity within the organization. The power figure usually surrounds himself with functional specialists to advise and to promote an image of omnipotence.

The organization often operates by subordinates guessing what the top wants, and then doing it. The grapevine is used to establish the wishes of those at the top and for obtaining feedback on subsequent action.

In a power culture, decisions tend to be made either autocratically or as a result of political fights. Though formal consensual procedures for decision making may exist, they tend to be bypassed.

Expertise is not the critical success factor for an individual to succeed in this culture; it is the extensive contacts, resources, status, and high visibility which an individual can offer which are paramount.

> Expertise is not the critical success factor for an individual to succeed in a power culture; it is the extensive contacts, resources, status, and high visibility which an individual can offer which are paramount.

The Murdoch media empire typifies a power culture. Rupert Murdoch rules his empire from the centre and employs functional specialists to promote and maintain his power base. He runs a tough, abrasive and competitive business where individuals are judged solely by their business performance. Rules, procedure, and committees are largely ignored in the Murdoch empire. As the then editor of the *Sun* newspaper, Kelvin MacKenzie, saw it: "... corporate relations and PR (were) bullshit. For him there were only two things that mattered – the readers, translated into sales figures and letters and phone calls to the paper, and the Boss".[19]

The multimillion pound Hanson commercial empire was dominated by the power and force of personality of James Hanson, now Lord Hanson. His biographers report that Hanson liked to sit at the center of the web which made up his empire and call the shots by issuing orders either directly to his executives or through his three secretaries. Executives were known to dread hearing his booming voice at the end of the phone or seeing him wander into their offices.[20]

When Harold Geneen took over ITT, he transformed it from a relatively comfortable and complacent company into one of the fastest growing and most profitable companies in America of the period. In large part he achieved this success by introducing a highly power-centered culture, with him at the core, supported by an aggressive central staff and tight financial systems.[21]

One of the key tools in Geneen's management style was the monthly divisional review meeting. Around 150 managers were invited to attend these meetings, seated around an oblong table, with microphones placed in front of them. These hapless managers were then subjected to intense and rapid questioning on the results they had achieved by members of Geneen's central staff. Geneen would sit at the head of the table, watching. At the first sign of weakness or lack of factual knowledge, he would pitch in and tear the manager to shreds. So intense was the pressure that many of the managers publicly broke down in tears.

■ Role culture

The role culture is the stereotypical bureaucratic organization, dominated by rules, procedures, and job specialization. Great emphasis is, therefore, placed on working through prescribed authority relationships, with formal communications procedures, but little contact between individuals outside of these. Individuals

DEFINITION

are expected to work solely within the confines of their job descriptions: performance beyond the role is not required and is indeed perceived as threatening.

It is the role (with its rules and procedures, together with the position power which it confers) which is the source of influence. In contrast to the power culture, any influence strategies which are out-of-role would be totally abhorrent.

The old IBM (International Business Machines), the fourth largest United States corporation, has traditionally had a highly rule-bound role culture.[22] In fact, IBM's founder, Thomas Watson, had rules for almost everything: dark business suits, white shirts, and striped ties were "the uniform." Drinking alcohol, even off the job, was prohibited. IBM actually dismissed a female employee for dating someone who worked for a competitor. And employees were required to accept such frequent transfers that insiders liked to say that IBM stood for "I've Been Moved." The rules are a little less severe today, but the conservative image is still alive.

The fast-food operation, McDonald's, is another strong example of a highly role-specific culture. Absolutely everything is specified – reward systems, policies, procedures, norms of behavior, burger cooking times, how to lay the food out on the plate, how to greet customers – to name but a few of the myriad rules and regulations constraining behavior.

■ Task culture

DEFINITION

The focus in a task culture is on the job or project. The organization employs groups of experts to focus on a particular task or issue. Power and influence derive from the expertise the individual holds, rather than from position or personal power. Because individuals work in teams, they tend to feel more powerful than if they were assigned to particular job roles. The teams themselves are emphasized within the organization, not the individual.

Applicants for positions at Compaq Computer, for example, are carefully chosen for their ability to fit into the company's team-work-oriented culture. As one executive put it: "We can find lots of people who are competent. ... The No. 1 issue is whether they fit into the way we do business".[23]

At Compaq, that means finding job candidates who are easy to get along with and who feel comfortable with the company's consensus management style. To increase the likelihood that loners and those with big egos get screened out, it is not unusual for an applicant to be interviewed by 15 people who represent all departments of the company and a variety of seniority levels.[24]

Competition between teams can sometimes emerge when resource allocation from top management is tight, and the culture may move to a role or power culture when the organization is in difficulty.

■ Person culture

> The person culture is somewhat rare. This culture is normally seen in organizations whose mission is to satisfy the creative or technical needs of the people involved, rather than any purposes of the organization itself. This type of culture is usually found in lawyers' offices, architectural partnerships, and some small consultancies. There is no formal hierarchical structure nor are there any formal control mechanisms, since these organizations tend to work by mutual consent. Influence tends to be shared and power will tend to be based on expertise.

DEFINITION

Sometimes a person culture coexists with a task or role culture. Professional staff may see their organization as a base from which to pursue their own professional interests. This is sometimes found in university institutions among the professorial staff.

Using influence and power among these types of people can be enormously difficult, because the services of such specialists are usually in demand and they can move position fairly easily.

Diagnosing culture – the tools

If you are to be successful at exerting influence in the system, you must develop the skills to identify which type of culture exists in your organization. Accurate diagnosis involves a number of tools, including:

- objectivity,
- who gets ahead?
- length of service,
- what's hidden behind the formality? and
- anecdotes and stories.[25]

■ Objectivity

As we discussed in chapter three, accurate perception requires that we forget our own values and assumptions about the right way of doing things. Instead, systems and situations must be evaluated objectively. If a manager uses his own values to interpret the organizational culture, he will inevitably miss what is important in the company, who gets ahead, which projects matter – in short, he will make a misdiagnosis. This will prove a stumbling block, because an organization's cultural values serve as an informal control system that tells people what is expected of them.

Think back to the case study of Laura: she misjudged the culture of her new organization by drawing on her own value system and assumptions about what was valued. She then displayed behavior which was totally inappropriate to the culture of her new organization.

■ Who gets ahead?

You must establish who gets ahead in the organization and why. Is it the macho gung-ho type; the sales person; or the person who knows the right people? This insight will reveal what the culture believes and values. Do people get ahead for their skills, length of service, or results achieved?

Without outside intervention, culture tends to be self-perpetuating. A manager who has been promoted because he does not rock the boat will probably promote people who are similar to himself; subsequently and consequently, others in the organization will copy that behavior.

John DeLorean was particularly critical of the General Motors's practice through the 1960s and 1970s which he described as the "promotion of the unobvious candidate."[26] Under this practice, the finance division built up a power base by promoting people who were not regarded as contenders for the post, as a way of creating a loyal, dependent, and committed group of managers who would do their sponsor's bidding, because they owed him a favor. For DeLorean, this practice merely symbolized the deterioration in General Motors's culture.

■ Length of service

In a culture where people stay in jobs a long time, they may not be particularly motivated to make an immediate impact. This again tells you something about what the culture values and believes in.

MCI reflects the belief of its founder, William McGowan, that neither seniority nor corporate loyalty is important. Pins in recognition of five years of service, or indeed ten, are non-existent, because they imply that people who have been with the company longer are somehow better. As McGowan says: "The opposite is almost always the truth. It's the newcomers, the young people, who bring the fresh ideas and the energy".[27]

In keeping with these values, MCI has an official goal of filling at least half of all job openings from the outside.

■ What's hidden behind the formality?

We saw from the discussion of Mintzberg's work in chapter one that managers spend a lot of time in meetings. Meetings undoubt-edly have formal agendas and minutes, but what is more impor-tant is the hidden agenda that gets played out. At a team meeting, do members of the team spar with each other? Is one team member vulnerable because an acquisition which he or she spon-sored is failing to produce the promised payback? Who rallies round to offer support to a colleague when the boss goes on the rampage? What is not discussed?

Also consider what the senior people spend their time writing about. Does a proposal from a subordinate for a major project receive a response from a superior requesting further (and insignificant) detail as a stalling tactic, or is the response one of congratulating the project's proposer for having suggested an additional initiative which will enhance the performance of the organization?

■ Anecdotes and stories

Deal and Kennedy suggest paying particular attention to the anec-dotes and stories which people in the organization share with one another. They argue that the same story told by many different people is particularly significant.[28]

They recommend that the influential manager should always seek out the point behind particular stories, since it will reveal invaluable information about behavior acceptable to the organi-zation. For example, such stories may indicate who the heroes are, whether macho management is in or out, whether customers are partners or dupes. One story told at 3M, for instance, tells how a worker was fired because he continued to work on a new product idea even after his boss had told him to stop. Despite being fired and taken off the payroll, the individual continued to come to work, pursuing his idea in an unused office. Eventually he was rehired, developed the idea into a huge success, and was made vice-president. This story promotes an important value in the innovative 3M culture – persisting when you believe an idea.[29]

Influence and networking

Understanding culture is the first stage in gaining access to the informal system, and it provides the influential manager with a guide to the kind of actions and behavior the organization is willing to accept. However, you can only begin to use this information successfully when you actively begin to work the informal system through the networking process.

"Networks," or interest groups, make up the heart of most organizations, particularly flat, interdependent organizations. Networks are one of the potential sources of power a manager must tap into in order to exercise influence effectively. Networks offer "connection power" – the more access you have to a wide range of personal and professional people inside and outside the organization, the greater your power and influence will be.

According to Arthur Schlesinger, Franklin D. Roosevelt was a consummate networker:

> "The first task of an executive, as Roosevelt saw it, was to guarantee himself an effective flow of information and ideas. ... Roosevelt's persistent effort, therefore, was to check and balance information acquired through official channels by information acquired through a myriad of private, informal, and unorthodox channels and espionage networks. At times, he seemed almost to pit his personal sources against his public sources."[30]

The benefits of networking to the influential manager are clear.

Most successful influence attempts are based on careful planning, on networks, and on persistent effort. Research was undertaken among more than 450 managers by Fred Luthans and his associates to discover whether the managers who are promoted most quickly through the organization perform the same activities and with the same emphasis as those managers who do the job most effectively.[31] It would be natural to

> Networks, or interest groups, make up the heart of most organizations, particularly flat, interdependent organizations. They are one of the potential sources of power a manager must tap into in order to exercise influence effectively.

> It would be natural to expect that speed of promotion is directly related to effective job performance, but this is not necessarily true.

expect that speed of promotion is directly related to effective job performance, but this is not necessarily true.

Figure 4 below shows that the most *successful* managers (in terms of speed of promotion) had a very different emphasis from *effective* managers (in terms of job performance). Networking is the most

Figure 4
Distribution of management time per activity

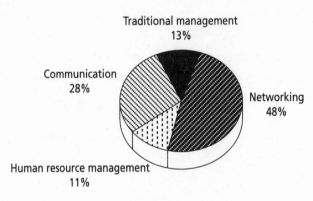

Successful managers

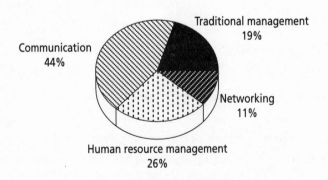

Effective managers

Source: Figure 3-2, Figure 4-2 from *Real Managers* by F. Luthans and R. M. Hodgetts and S. A. Rosenkrantz. Copyright © 1988 by Ballinger Publishing Company. Reprinted by permission of HarperCollins Publishers Inc.

important element in gaining promotion, human resource management the least important. In contrast, for effective managers, communication came top of the list, networking at the bottom. This study illustrates beyond doubt the central importance of networking skills in getting ahead in organizations.

> **Luthans's research defined networking as an activity encompassing socializing/politicking and interacting with outsiders.**
>
> **Socializing/politicking included nonwork-related "chit-chat;" informal joking around; discussing rumors; complaining, griping, and putting others down; politicking and gamesmanship.**
>
> **Interacting with outsiders included dealing with customers and suppliers; public relations; attending external meetings; and attending community service events.[32]**

DEFINITION

> The top managers in Mintzberg's famous study were followed around for one week and everything they did was recorded. Mintzberg found that they relied heavily on verbal contacts and networking in order to function effectively. The network of contacts in the study included superiors, subordinates, peers, and other individuals inside the organization, as well as numerous outsiders. Some of the contacts were personal, such as friends and peers. Others were professional, such as consultants, lawyers, and insurance underwriters. Still others were trade association contacts, customers, and suppliers. This research strongly supports the notion that managers need to develop a major network of contacts in order to have influence and to operate effectively.[33]

RECENT FINDINGS

Networking can create power and influence for departments within the organization. It is rare, for example, that human resources departments exert much power in organizations.[34] There are exceptions, of course – at a time when Apple Computers was dominated by engineers, marketers, finance, and sales people, Apple's human resources department developed a network of contacts right across the different divisions of the company, precisely at a time when these divisions were fighting one another:

> "Because they headed a network that extended into every crevice of the organization, Jay Elliot and Mary Fortney ... knew everything that was going on – who was unhappy, who was jealous, and who was saying what to whom. ... The meetings were thoroughly scripted and HR had the script. Mary was a facilitator ... guiding the process, like the psychologist who stays in the background but exerts control with the subtle and well-timed remark".[35]

Managers often trade power and the ability to get things done through networks. Their goal is to build strong reciprocal relationships so that when a manager has an immediate need, sufficient obligation exists to ensure fast cooperation.

Consider the example referred to by Robert Kaplan when describing a newly appointed manager of corporate employee relations:

> "I wanted a base that was different from what the groups reporting to me had and also from what my superiors had, so I established a series of contacts in other American industries until I knew on a first-name basis my counterpart at IBM, TRW, Procter and Gamble, Dupont, and General Electric, and I could get their input – input which the people in my organization didn't have."[36]

Kaplan compares the strengthening of lateral relationships in the organization to the establishment of trade routes in international trade. He suggests that networks of trading partners must be maintained and built every time the manager changes job.

Networks are usually determined by the values and objectives of its members. To a large extent, networks are built around the similarity principle, which is the fifth of our *six principles of influence* discussed in chapter two. Birds of a feather tend to flock together in networks, that is, people tend to associate with others like themselves for the purposes of debate and the exchange of information.

Networks can cover relationships inside and outside the organization. The general managers in John Kotter's study dedicated at least their first six months on the job to developing their networks both inside and outside the organization.[37] They recognized that strong networks were prerequisites for the successful implementation of their agendas. They were single-minded in forging relationships with anyone whom they thought had the potential to help them in the future.

There are different types of networks and various ways of classifying them. Let us now turn to a discussion of some of the more common networks which potential influencers may need to access and work through to achieve their influence objectives.

Types of network

■ Practitioner networks

Practitioner networks are groups of professional people who meet to debate issues of common professional interest. These networks could be either *formal*, such as a trade association based on marketing or manufacturing, or *informal*, such as women in the law.

In the mid-1990s, professional workers numbered some 20 percent of the USA's workforce, giving some idea of the potentially enormous influence of professional networks.[38]

DEFINITION

The role of *formal networks* includes lobbying, controlling the quality of the practitioners by stipulating entry criteria and providing ongoing training and development. The role of the *informal networks* includes information exchange, contact building, professional development, and intellectual stimulus.

Consider the case of Rupert Murdoch, outwardly the archetypal, omnipotent employer. For a significant period of time, however, he was unable to get rid of a troublesome, junior journalist on one of his many newspapers. That the journalist was

Father (union leader) of the relevant National Union of Journalists (NUJ) chapel was only part of the story. Equally important, perhaps, was the fact that the journalist's brother carried weight in the print union of another paper which Murdoch had targeted for acquisition.[39]

■ Exclusive power networks

DEFINITION

"If you have to ask the price, you should not be shopping here" – exclusive power networks are the exclusive province of those who already wield significant personal power and who wish to mix with their peers in order to further enhance and perpetuate it.

Meritocracy and equal opportunity are out. Elitism, personal contact, and introduction are in. You don't apply – you are invited to join. It is a network dominated either by the ties of friendship or those of the *alma mater*.

Caro's biography of the early years of Lyndon Johnson shows the important role played by personal contacts during his acquisition of Washington influence. While he was still Richard Kleberg's congressional secretary, Johnson gained access to privileged power networks by cultivating the friendship and acquaintance of power figures in the Roosevelt Administration:

"Not only … did Johnson know powerful officials who were in a position to help him, these officials knew him … and wanted to help him. A measure of this feeling was the number of patronage jobs Johnson obtained. … Such jobs were generally rationed … on the basis of a Congressman's importance. The office of the average Congressman might be given four or five, the office of a senior … Congressman perhaps twenty. … The office of Richard Kleberg, a Congressman with neither seniority nor power, was given fifty".[40]

■ Ideological networks

DEFINITION

Ideological networks tend to be spontaneous reactions to specific events and to draw from a very broad, disparate range of members. These events may be in the area of politics, environmental-

ism, social issues, or global business. Their objectives are to engi-
neer change.

Powerful recent examples of ideological networks include the
worldwide boycott of French food in protest against France's
nuclear testing; the boycott of Shell gasoline in response to that
company's proposal to dump at sea the Brent Spar oil rig; and the
recent French demonstrations against the French prime minister's
proposals to reform the public sector.

There is often agreement within the network as to the desired
outcome – this is often accompanied by conflict about the actual
means needed to achieve it.

Diagnosing networks – the tools for entry

■ Accessing networks

To be influential in the 1990s, you must access networks, and once in them, start to cultivate them.
The movement toward what Charles Savage terms
"fifth generation management"[41] is so rapid – away
from the old steep hierarchies toward flatter networking organizations – that it is now true to say:
"no network, no influence."

> There is no automatic entry into networks, but there are two important processes which must be followed: (1) target the network gatekeeper; (2) ensure that you fit in with the norms of the network.

Being in a network will give you information not
only on "what" needs to be done, equally importantly, it will also
provide insights into the "how." There is no automatic entry into
networks, but there are two important processes which must be
followed: (1) target the network gatekeeper; (2) ensure that you
fit in with the norms of the network.

■ Target the network gatekeeper

Every network has a gatekeeper who controls access to it. Gate-keepers can act as sponsors for potential entrants. Getting one to sponsor you, getting in by the back door, as it were, is an excellent shortcut mechanism for becoming a member.

Going back to our earlier example of Lyndon Johnson, his rise during the early years was due in large part to his cultivation of one man, Sam Rayburn. Rayburn's gatekeeper role gave Johnson access to informal gatherings among very powerful and senior congressmen and the political establishment generally. As the friend of such a powerful person, Johnson soon became a formidable figure himself, to be treated with deference.

■ Fit in with the network norms

Rather like an exclusive London club, networks have rules and norms which are sacrosanct and which members contravene at the cost of being isolated at best, thrown out at worst.

Michael Heseltine (the British prime minister who never was) is a classic example of a person whose driving goal was thwarted in large part because he failed to adhere to the network norms, as his biographer Julian Critchley makes clear:

> "Michael neglects the House of Commons. His public profile may be high, but his attendance in the smoking-room is an event to be remarked upon. ... To how many of his colleagues ... he could put a name is anyone's guess. ... There was always something splendid about Michael's isolation, a condition brought on in part by temperament and in part by pride. ... [As] Michael said, 'I'm not a very clubbable person – sitting around with a drink and people coming up to you. That kind of getting-to-know-how-you-tick is a time-consuming exercise. I do have a considerable workload ...'"[42]

■ Building influence within and through the network

The core skills and qualities required by the influential manager concern the process of cooperation or, as social psychologists term it, "reciprocity." You must learn how to trade with people within the network so that you can build up credits and subsequently cash in on them. You should also understand how you can exchange different currencies with different people. The five types of potentially tradeable currencies identified by Allan Cohen and David Bradford are:

- inspiration-related,
- task-related,
- position-related,
- relationship-related, and
- personal-related.

These are explained in detail in Figure 5 overleaf.[43] Whatever currency you decide to use, your objective must be to develop a critical mass of people willing and able to support the case for your influence objective.

■ Accessing the grapevine

Networks of all types and varieties can be also be accessed by the "grapevine" or, as social psychologists call it, "the organization's unofficial communication network." Managers who wish to be influential need to keep their ears open to grapevine information, although they will probably not be part of it themselves. Access to the grapevine will help you pick up important information which may affect potential attempts at using influence; it may also allow you to test out a particular idea or proposal.

Grapevines are a useful source of personal insight into your potential targets. Consider Walter Wriston, the corporate leader who transformed First National Citibank into Citicorp – one of

Figure 5
Commonly traded organizational currencies

Inspiration-related currencies

Vision	Being involved in a task that has larger significance for the unit, organization, customers, or society.
Excellence	Having a chance to do important things really well.
Moral/ethical correctness	Doing what is "right" by a higher standard than efficiency.

Task-related currencies

Resources	Lending or giving money, budget increases, personnel, space, and so forth.
Assistance	Helping with existing projects or undertaking unwanted tasks.
Cooperation	Giving task support, providing quicker response time, approving a project, or aiding implementation.
Information	Providing organizational as well as technical knowledge.

Position-related currencies

Advancement	Giving a task or assignment that can aid in promotion.
Recognition	Acknowledging effort, accomplishment, or abilities.
Visibility	Providing chance to be known by higher-ups or significant others in the organization.
Reputation	Enhancing the way a person is seen.
Importance/insiderness	Offering a sense of importance, of "belonging."
Network/contacts	Providing opportunities for linking with others.

Relationship-related currencies

Acceptance/inclusion	Providing closeness and friendship.
Personal support	Giving personal and emotional backing.
Understanding	Listening to others' concerns and issues.

Personal-related currencies

Self-concept	Affirming one's values, self-esteem, and identity.
Challenge/learning	Sharing tasks that increase skills and abilities.
Ownership/involvement	Letting others have ownership and influence.
Gratitude	Expressing appreciation or indebtedness.

the pre-eminent financial institutions in the world. Wriston was a master at building informal intelligence networks, as fellow executive Harry Levinson described:

> "He relies very heavily on information that comes to him from different parts of the organization. He gets and absorbs the feelings of people who are not only Department and Group heads but always has a wary ear open to be alert to situations, circumstances within the shop that might not surface in the ordinary routine of management information flows. ... He's got a very acute sense ... of the ideas as they float around the organization".[44]

Wriston was so aware of the dangers of being out of touch that, according to a *Financial World* interview, he specifically warned Jack Welch of the problem when the latter took over at GE.[45] He explained how the man at the top is normally the last to know the critical details – the grapevine allows him to be among the first. Wriston's advice applies to all managers, not just those at the top. Without access to the network of communication provided by the grapevine, you are destined to be always out of touch.

■ Moles and mouths

Managers can access the grapevine through intermediaries, referred to as "moles" and "mouths."

> Moles listen. They relay information back to managers. Their status is normally executive level, but crucially they enjoy the easy everyday access to the workforce which their more senior masters do not. Moles are no different to spies – their best work is done undercover when nobody knows for whom they work.

DEFINITION

UK government ministers use their parliamentary private secretaries (PPSs) to access the political grapevine. In illustration, as Julian Critchley drily notes:

> "A minister's isolation is not total. In recent years even the most obscure have been given Parliamentary Private Secretaries. ... The

task of the PPS is to add tonic to his masters's gin, help him on with his overcoat, and keep him informed".[46]

Moles can often be the power behind the throne because they have the ear of the boss. The classic example of a mole or "whisper" is Harry Bennett, the director of security for Ford in the latter period of Henry Ford, Senior. Over the years, Bennett ingratiated himself with the elder Ford and built a network of spies and enforcers throughout the company. Bennett became so powerful that as Ford reached his late seventies and his health began to decline, Bennett conceived and executed schemes to remove from power all other senior managers who were not personally loyal to the security chief. Only the active intervention of Clara Ford (Henry's wife) and the widow of Edsel Ford, prevented Bennett from taking over the company completely. His bitter comment to Henry Ford II on the day that the latter was installed as president was: "You're taking over a billion-dollar organization here that you haven't contributed a thing to!"[47]

DEFINITION

If moles listen, mouths transmit. They are ideal if you want to float a proposal informally to evaluate its likely reception when launched formally. If the initial reception to the leaked proposal is favorable, you can swiftly proceed to formal launch. Should the initial reception be unfavorable, you simply keep quiet, and deny any responsibility for the idea, should the need arise. You will find mouths everywhere: in the boardroom, typing pool, and even on the shopfloor.

Lord Donoughue was one of Harold Wilson's main advisors between 1974 and 1979 and has been likened to an Elizabethan courtier.[48] His great skill was trading information, bartering what he knew in exchange for what others knew, building up in the process a network of confidants. He thus created a reputation for being in the know and for having an influence, even when by his own admission, it was something that he did not always have.

Networks are a powerful force in and around organizations. Every company has them, no matter how small the company.

Managers cannot afford to ignore networks. They must use them to make things happen.

CHAPTER SUMMARY

- This chapter has focussed on the significant relationship between the hidden system of the organization and successful influencing behavior.

- It has examined organizational culture and organizational networks as the prime components of this hidden system.

- We saw how culture serves as an unwritten guide to the kinds of influencing behavior which the organization is willing to accept.

- Human networks are the channels through which we use the information gathered, in order to actively work the informal system.

CONCEPT QUIZ

Do you understand the hidden system of your organization and its impact on the successful use of influence? Answer the following questions to test your understanding:

1. The best results are always achieved by following the proper channels of authority. *True or false?*

2. The influential manager ignores the myths and stories which circulate in the organization. *True or false?*

3. Managers can unleash influence by building relationships which focus on people's emotions and feelings, the so-called "soft side" of organizational life. *True or false?*

4. Organizational culture is an unwritten guide to the kinds of influencing behavior acceptable in different organizations. *True or false?*

5. Managers have to develop the skill and ability to understand and diagnose their own culture if they are to be successful influencers. *True or false?*

6. Human networks are a central route through which we can begin to work the informal system. *True or false?*

7. Networks are a potent source of connection power. *True or false?*

8. Networking makes the biggest single relative contribution to a manager's promotional success. *True or false?*

9. Networks are usually determined by the values and objectives of its members. *True or false?*

10. Networks allow the influential manager to activate the similarity principle, that is, "birds of a feather flock together." *True or false?*

Answers

1(F), 2(F), 3(T), 4(T), 5(T), 6(T), 7(T), 8(T), 9(T), 10(T).

ACTIVATING THE HIDDEN SYSTEM

FEATURE
CASE
STUDY

Although Laura had been mistaken in her belief that James was a ratio-nal, results-driven manager like herself, she decided to put those mis-takes behind her and embark on a thorough revision of her strategy for handling James and the rest of the company.

She knew that the first thing she had to do was to forget her own value system as to what constituted good, professional management practice. She would begin to work to what was acceptable and valued by the com-pany for which she was working.

Laura decided to try out her new strategy on a particular proposal on which she wanted agreement. This proposal was to make Ron Butler redundant; he was a technically unqualified quality control and customer care manager, who was unwilling to upgrade his professional skills.

Laura now realized that if she presented purely rational criteria to James, such as the damage wrought on company profitability by poor product quality and by low customer service levels, James would not be convinced. Instead, Laura had to devise a strategy which would allow James to come to the conclusion independently of his rather cerebral marketing director.

Accordingly, Laura planned a strategy to use third-party sources as conduits through which to leak the information on Butler. Laura remembered reading during her MBA course something about the power of the grapevine and moles and mouths, although she had thought at the time that this sounded more like a Jeffrey Archer novel than effective management practice.

But Laura set out to activate her network of contacts both inside and outside the organization who were in touch with James. She would use them to pass information on to James, and thereby sow the seeds of doubt in his mind.

One of her prime leakage points was James's own secretary, Cassan-dra. She disliked the fact that Ron went out drinking at lunchtime and often flirted with her on his return to the office. She was only too recep-tive when Laura told her, in strictest confidence of course, that she had had to institute formal disciplinary proceedings against Butler for his drinking when a liquid lunch had led to him being offhand with a key customer.

The next time that James asked Cassandra to remind him to ring Butler for information on product reject levels, she said, "Just a tip, James, if you want accurate figures, I'd ring before lunch, if I were you." James was concerned: officers drinking in the wardroom after dinner was one thing, but during the day when in charge of the ratings was something else. ...

Similarly, Laura planted information with a managing director contact in another company, known to James through a trade association. Laura told this mutual acquaintance, Philip, about a recent incident involving an order for their largest customer. A sharp-eyed member of the despatch department had spotted a product fault in the order as it was about to be despatched. In accordance with procedures, a stop was placed on the order and Butler was advised. For reasons best known to himself, Butler refused point blank to become involved and instructed despatch to ship all the goods, whatever the quality, saying: "On no account tell the marketing people," and "Let's just deny all knowledge." What was worse, Laura had heard on the grapevine that this long-standing customer had since decided to put his business out to tender.

When Philip related this story about Butler to James, James was staggered that a man whom he considered to be officer material was prepared to endanger the livelihood of his own men by so wanton an act.

At the next marketing meeting, James asked Laura if the changes she had introduced had caused Butler to lose his sea legs. Laura replied, "Yes, I've heard some mutterings from the crew, but ..." James interrupted, "Absolutely understood, enough said, we need to clear the decks as far as Butler is concerned. Good man in his time, but just can't hack it any longer."

Laura smiled inwardly and said to herself that there really was something to this organizational behavior material after all.

Review question

1. What did Laura do right this time?

SUMMARY CHECKLIST

❑ Always stringently analyze the organizational culture.

❑ Match your behavior in attempting to use influence to suit the norms, values, and beliefs of your organization's culture.

❑ Avoid relying only on formal channels and systems to influence others.

❑ Actively build and develop networks by use of the similarity principle.

❑ Remember to actively trade information to be able to exercise influence within your network.

ACTION CHECKLIST

1. Review a situation where you have tried to use influence through formal, rational means alone. How successful was this strategy?

_____

_____

2. Reflect on a situation where you have rationally understood the need for a decision, but felt different emotionally. Consider how you might have reacted if the third party had thought about your feelings and emotions as well as the rational criteria.

_____

_____

3. Consider the current environment of your organization objectively and reflect on how well your behavior matches its norms, values, and beliefs as to the appropriate behavior.

_____

_____

4. Identify your current network of contacts and consider how you might begin to actively widen your circle, both inside and outside the organization.

_____

_____

5. Attempt to identify the gatekeepers who can give you access to new networks.

_____

_____

6. Identify the values to which the network adheres and how far you can match your behavior to suit them.

_____

_____

7. Attempt to get liked by, and ingratiate yourself to, the people within your networks.

_____

_____

8. Begin to build contacts with people across, up, and down the organization who can act as your moles and mouths.

_____

_____

9. Actively build your information base by keeping your ears open to grapevine gossip.

_____

_____

10. Identify and initiate a proposal on which you need to gain approval through your network of contacts.

_____

_____

chapter
six

STEP FOUR – DECIDE ON STRATEGY AND TACTICS

This chapter focuses on the need for a systematic understanding of the tactics and strategies of influence.

It examines the eight tactical weapons of influence open to the influential manager and how they might be applied. It looks at the effectiveness of different tactics and the need to match specific tactics to specific objectives and targets. The chapter compares the tactics usually deployed when influencing the boss, peer group, and subordinates.

It stresses the importance of using multiple influence tactics for the critical attempts at using influence.

Tactics are then classified into *soft* or *strong* strategies of influence. Soft strategies have been shown to be generally more effective, given the flatter nature of today's organizations and the individual's psychological response to the process of influence.

In conclusion, the chapter presents a typology of managers with varying levels of skill in exercising influence.

SELF-ASSESSMENT EXERCISE

Implementing the eight tactical weapons of influence

The following short quiz is designed to help you assess your personal understanding and use of the eight tactical weapons of influence.

Read the following list of influence strategies and answer "yes" or "no" as they apply to your current situation.

1. Do you ever involve people you wish to influence in the decision-making process? *Yes or no?*

2. Do you ever use demands, threats, or intimidation to get people to comply with a request? *Yes or no?*

3. Do you ever appeal to higher authority when you are trying to persuade someone to accept your proposal – for example, do you claim that "the Board insists that …"? *Yes or no?*

4. Do you offer the idea of some future reward when you are seeking to persuade someone to support your proposal? *Yes or no?*

5. Do you ever canvass the aid of other people to support your position when you make a proposal to your boss or peers? *Yes or no?*

6. Do you ever try to flatter your target and make him or her feel good prior to making a request? *Yes or no?*

7. Do you ever use data and facts to persuade other people of the merits of your proposal? *Yes or no?*

8. Do you ever make emotional appeals, e.g. by evoking a vision of a better future, to arouse enthusiasm for, and commitment to, your ideas? *Yes or no?*

Follow-up

These eight approaches are representative of the various tactical weapons of influence that we will discuss in this chapter. A manager who has answered "yes" to four or more is likely to have a reasonably effective range of influence tactics at his or her disposal.

"Yes" answers numbering three or less, indicate a need to considerably broaden the repertoire of weapons at the manager's disposal because it is likely that he or she is experiencing fairly high rates of failure in exercising influence.

"No" answers to all of the statements, indicate someone currently living the life of an organizational hermit who possesses no influence in his or her organization.

The need for systematic influence

Up to this point, we have examined the steps which lead up to the influence process, such as self-knowledge, values, goals, and objectives, insight into your target's world, and matching your behavior to the target's comfort zone.

We have also stressed the importance of understanding the hidden system in the organization, its culture, the norms of behavior, and the informal human networks which are interwoven with its formal hierarchy.

The next logical step is to discuss the various influence tactics and strategies which you can deploy to successfully persuade other people to voluntarily change their attitudes toward events, people, and decisions so that your ideas are implemented.

Although the exercise of influence is a fundamental activity in all organizations, particularly in the flat interdependent organizations of the 1990s, only a few authors have systematically identified influence tactics from formal research. Instead, much of the advice in the current management literature is restricted to anecdotal tips on managerial tactics such as, "the manager should use compliments and flattery to ingratiate himself with his boss" or "facts and figures are the best tools of persuasion."

While such anecdotal tips undoubtedly have a use, this armchair speculation does not systematically inform managers about the full range of tactics open to them. It fails to explain how to match tactics to the situation and to the influence objectives.

Recent research by Gary Yukl and Cecilia Falbe indicates, however, that there are eight, standardized ways by which managers attempt to get what they want.[1] And as with the rest of this book, this chapter draws upon this area of psychological research to help you employ the standardized strategies and tactics in your quest to become an influential manager.

The eight tactical weapons of influence

When managers were asked to complete questionnaires on the influence tactics they used to influence their bosses, co-workers, or subordinates, a total of eight commonly found influence tactics were identified in today's organizations. These we shall call the eight tactical weapons of influence, and they are: (1) pressure tactics, (2) upward appeals, (3) exchange, (4) coalitions, (5) ingratiation, (6) rational persuasion, (7) inspirational appeals, and (8) consultation. We will consider each of these in detail.

■ Tactic 1: Pressure

According to Yukl and Falbe, pressure tactics influence the target by using demands, threats or intimidation.[2]

Types of pressure tactic identified by David Kipnis *et al.* included the manager constantly checking up on the target, ordering the target to fulfill his requests, shouting or bawling at the target, setting aggressive deadlines, pestering the individual until the work was done, expressing anger verbally, provoking a face-to-face showdown, or spelling out the rules which required that the target do as he was told.[3]

Kelvin MacKenzie of the *Sun* newspaper was such a master pressure tactician that he was nicknamed "Mac the Knife":[4]

"Bollockings as standard management technique began at the start of the day when MacKenzie went through the features page which had been prepared the day before. ... Picking a page he would run his eye over it, ringing paragraphs with his fat green pen. 'That's crap!' he would spit. The pen would move off across the page again. 'And that's crap!' Another paragraph, or a whole article, would be ringed. ... The scrutiny would continue, from headline down to the smallest article or detail of punctuation. ... He was anywhere and everywhere, picking out every weakness."[5]

Harold Geneen of ITT was well known for intimidating his managers in the monthly financial performance meetings. DeLorean
tells of a General Motors executive who got his way because he
was ugly and mean-looking and intimidated others.

Alan Sugar, chairman of Amstrad, is well-known for his use of
pressure tactics, which became unacceptable to his chief executive, David Rogers, who resigned significantly before the end of
his contract:

> "Alan Sugar, chairman of Amstrad, used to have his hair and trade-
> mark badger beard trimmed in a small hairdressing salon in Brent-
> wood, Essex, close to his company's spartan headquarters.
>
> "But recently he has not been welcomed. Sugar's abrasive and
> often ill-tempered style – well-known to the City's investors and ana-
> lysts – proved too much for his hairdressers.
>
> "Evidently the combative traits of the Amstrad founder and Tot-
> tenham Hotspur chairman were also unacceptable to his chief execu-
> tive, David Rogers. After seeing out only 16 months of a three-year
> contract, Rogers announced … he would be leaving Amstrad …"[6]

The ploy of exploiting time pressure evokes principle three, the
scarcity principle – things are perceived according to how scarce
they are. A tight deadline always creates a sense of urgency and a
momentum in favor of the person presenting the time-sensitive
proposal. Equally, a proposal deliberately presented close to the
deadline reduces the time to debate either its acceptability or the
method by which it might be accomplished.

Deadlines also induce the anxiety that the opportunity to take
advantage of a proposal may be lost. During spring 1996 when a
Labour Party victory at the next national election
appeared highly possible, the incumbent UK Conservative government used the forthcoming election to exert time pressure to force through
privatization of the railway system, suggesting to
interested parties that the opportunity might be lost
were it not exploited immediately.

The opposite use of time pressure as a tactic is

> The ploy of exploiting time
> pressure evokes principle three,
> the scarcity principle. … A tight
> deadline always creates a sense
> of urgency and a momentum in
> favor of the person presenting
> the time-sensitive proposal.

delay – the waiting game. Causing others to wait is a tactic that can increase your influence just as much as forcing the pace on a particular issue. As head of Standard Brands, Ross Johnson developed a personal style which helped him exercise power, including what he termed "the grand entrance": "Johnson arrived twenty minutes late, punctually, to everything. 'If you're on time, no-one notices you,' he would say. 'If you are late, they pay attention.'"[7]

> The opposite use of time as a pressure tactic is delay – the waiting game.

■ Tactic 2: Upward appeals

Yukl and Falbe report that upward appeals either involve the manager seeking to persuade the target that the request is approved by higher management, or appealing to higher management for assistance in gaining the target's compliance with the request.[8]

Kipnis *et al.* cite the tactics of formally appealing to someone in higher management to back up a request; gaining the informal support of people in higher positions; sending a memo about another person to higher echelons; or perhaps sending a subordinate or peer to see someone higher up to convince that person of the merit of your view or proposal.[9]

Upward appeals activate the authority of the formal position of the boss, using the boss as a source of social proof. The strategy of saying "the boss wants this" or "headquarters won't like that" is frequently used and rarely questioned.

The general managers in John Kotter's famous study[10] often called upon their immediate boss, even sometimes bosses two or three levels up the organization, to help them implement their agendas. Suppliers, customers, even competitors, were used to appeal to those underneath them to follow their agendas.

■ Tactic 3: Exchange

Under the terms of exchange perceived by Yukl and Falbe, the influential manager may promise, either explicitly or implicitly, that the target will be rewarded for agreeing to the manager's request for action; alternatively, the manager may remind the target of a favour yet to be repaid.[11]

Exchange tactics capitalize on what academics call "the norm of reciprocity," which states that we are obligated to future repayment of favors, gifts, invitations, and so forth.[12] The general managers in Kotter's study[13] would sometimes trade the resources available to them to achieve their agendas.

It is instructive to examine a real-life example. As president of Nabisco Brands, Ross Johnson apparently deferred to the CEO and chairman, Robert Schaeberle, at every opportunity. Not content with constantly addressing Schaeberle as "Mr Chairman" in meetings and ensuring that the company paid his country club subscription, Johnson authorized Nabisco company funds to endow a university chair in accounting in Schaeberle's name. So effective were these exchange tactics that Johnson was elevated to chief executive.[14]

Brummer and Cowe[15] record how Lord Hanson made full use of exchange tactics with whatever political party was in power in order to ensure that his empire was the first to be consulted whenever there was a business opportunity or government-related deal. In the 1960s, Hanson had a close working relationship with a fellow native of Huddersfield: Harold Wilson. When the Huddersfield authorities suggested making a statue of Hanson the centerpiece of their civic redevelopment program in 1989, Hanson wrote to the local newspaper counterproposing Harold Wilson, and argued that Huddersfield should honor its first prime minister instead of its biggest industrial tycoon. Notwithstanding this relationship with the Labour Party, Hanson became the second largest benefactor to Conservative Party causes and to Mrs Thatcher's favorite think-tank – The Centre for Policy Studies – in the 1980s.

> Exchange tactics capitalize on what academics call the "norm of reciprocity," which states that we are obligated to future repayment of favors, gifts, invitations, and so forth.

■ Tactic 4: Coalitions

With the coalition tactics described by Yukl and Falbe, the manager either gets others to persuade the target, or directly persuades the target that because others support the manager, the target should too.[16]

The power of tapping into the hidden system of informal networks to create coalitions of support was discussed extensively in chapter five. Coalitions help a manager to build a personal power base to support his or her demands and to activate the liking principle.

The flatter structure of contemporary organizations heightens the importance of interdependence while downgrading positional power. This means that you need allies upon whose trusting support you can count. Pfeffer goes so far as to call coalition tactics "the new golden rule."[17]

> With coalition tactics, the manager either gets others to persuade the target, or directly persuades the target that because others support the manager, the target should too.

Coalitions can be built in a number of different ways. One of the more obvious is to give positions of power to those people who demonstrate loyalty to you – Kelvin MacKenzie had his own particular preference for how that loyalty should be shown:

"True to the code of sarff [south] London, MacKenzie also wanted to be surrounded by 'made men,' who had proved themselves by pulling off some outrageous stunt at the expense of the opposition. One way of becoming a 'made man' was to phone the *Mirror* and ask for the 'stone' where the final versions of pages were assembled for the presses. The trick was to imitate another member of the *Mirror* staff to fool the stone sub into revealing the front-page splash. One features exec became a 'made man' by walking across Fleet Street into the *Express* and stealing some crucial pictures from the library. Hacks refusing to get involved in this sort of behavior were suspect – falling into the category of those who were not fully with him, and could therefore be presumed to be against him."[18]

Coalition tactics allow social consensus to be developed around a particular issue or particular person. Astute managers use such tactics to control their information environment so that it appears that everyone agrees with what they are doing or that they are the right people for the job.

An excellent example of creating a coalition of support to convince his target that he was the right person for the job can be found in the efforts of Henry Kissinger. A major factor in his appointment as special assistant for national security affairs in the first Nixon administration was his cultivation of influential contacts who would say good things of him to the new President, whether Nixon's campaign coordinator for foreign policy research, Richard Allen; newspaperman Joseph Kraft; or Nixon's deputy campaign manager, Peter M. Flanigan.[19]

■ Tactic 5: Ingratiation

Yukl and Falbe define ingratiating tactics as when influential managers seek to put the target in a good mood or to think positively of them before making a request.[20] This tactic builds heavily on the principle of "liking and ingratiation" – we like those people who like us and who express positive sentiments toward us, and we are correspondingly more likely to do things for them.

Kipnis *et al.* identify several ploys which the influencer wishing to exercise ingratiation may use.[21] It may be as simple as saying to the target "Only you have the brains and talent to do this" in order to make the target feel important. Similarly, the influencer may act in a very friendly or humble way prior to, or while, making a request. The influencer may not make the request until the target appears to be in a receptive mood. Alternatively, the influencer may praise the target or perhaps sympathise about the extra work that the request will cause.

Many of Mrs Thatcher's Cabinet appointees were noted as much for their skill at ingratiation as for their political or intellectual expertise. John Selwyn Gummer's elevation to party chairman and the promotion of Cecil Parkinson were seen by some commentators as the appointments of men born to please more than to act. As Andrew Thomson notes:

> "The old public-school Conservative often simply does not understand the female of the species. They fail to appreciate that this Prime Minister needs to be treated as a woman and not – and this is the crucial difference – with the apologetic approach of someone who wishes she were a man. The success of Cecil Parkinson is in some measure due to his ability to appreciate and understand that she is a woman as well as a Prime Minister."[22]

Many of the leading capitalists of the 1980s were characterized by their skillful use of charm to win influence and power, as the biographer Tom Bower comments:

> "All three, Murdoch, Goldsmith and Rowland, possessed wealth which had been used to buy an image of respectable, family-loving citizens, but in substance they were amoral, shrewd pirates. In common, they could charm adversaries to serve their purpose in a manner which victims and critics castigated as manipulation."[23]

Tiny Rowland's ingratiation into the good books of Dr Hastings Banda, the future Prime Minister of Malawi, is a case in point:

> "... Banda liked Rowland's style. His politeness, Banda noticed, was natural and not condescending. He used the word 'Sir' with charm. Subtly, Rowland hinted that he shared a bond with Banda and understood the black man's struggle. Like Banda, he too had been imprisoned by the British and suffered the sense of outrage, injustice and grievances of liberty denied by arrogant and heartless officials. This empathy appealed to Banda ..."[24]

This strategy of ingratiation masked Rowland's true feelings about Banda:

> "... Rowland complained to his friends that he was 'thoroughly fed up' with Banda's demands. ... He chuckled when told that at a public dinner, 'Banda sounded more like Peter Sellers imitating Adolf Hitler than ever.'
>
> "'If you think that I like sitting on the couch with Banda close up

to me,' Rowland told George Abindor on his return to Salisbury, 'spitting into my face as he talks, you must be mad. But it's business.'"[25]

By contrast, lack of the skills to ingratiate and to encourage liking explains how it was possible that in 1985, Steve Jobs, the co-founder of Apple Computer and one of its major stockholders, was forced out of all but a ceremonial position in the company.[26] This lack of skills is demonstrated by how Jobs dealt with a senior executive, Del Yocam, who ran the Apple II division and headed-up operations and manufacturing:

> "He went for a long walk around the parking lot with Del, and Del seemed to be agreeing with a lot of what he was saying. At a certain point, however, Steve was just unable to stop himself. He said he wanted to run operations, and he informed Del that he really was a much better operations person than Del was. ... Del asked him to repeat what he'd just said, so he did. After all, he was just repeating what should have been plain to everyone. But it wasn't plain to Del. Del was upset."[27]

■ Tactic 6: Rational persuasion

Drawing on Yukl and Falbe, we see that this tactic puts logical argument and facts center-stage – proposals are supported by rational evidence that they will succeed. Such evidence is also a powerful source of social proof.[28]

As Kipnis *et al.* point out, influential managers may use a detailed plan to justify their ideas, present factual information and logical analysis in support, or they may detail the background reasons for the request.[29] Before making the request, they may even demonstrate their competence and expertise to the target.

Take as an example the rational persuasion technique used by a plant manager to prevent a cutback in his workforce when the army phased out one of its tanks:

> "First the plant manager sold a new product line to divisional staff who reported to his boss. In the meantime he developed a presenta-

tion in the form of a comparative analysis showing the pros and cons of taking on the new product line. Ideas presented included such things as the reduced burden on other products, risk reward factors, and good community relations from the layoff avoided. The presentation was polished, written on viewgraphs, and presented in person. The plant manager made certain that his technical staff would be at the meeting ready to answer any questions that might damage the strength of the presentation."[30]

The rational use of facts presents an appearance of a scientific approach to decision making – and thus fits the image sought by many organizations – but it is important to remember Peter Drucker's famous dictum that anyone over the age of 21 can find the facts to support his or her position. After all, how often have you observed information and analysis being gathered retrospectively to ratify a decision that has already been made for quite different reasons?

Margaret Thatcher always armed herself with the facts and figures to secure her objectives, as Andrew Thomson observed:

> **The rational use of facts presents an appearance of a scientific approach to decision making – and thus fits the image sought by many organizations – but it is important to remember Peter Drucker's famous dictum that anyone over the age of 21 can find facts to support his or her position.**

"Her appetite for statistics was to prove insatiable. When she was appointed to the Shadow Cabinet and was used by Edward Heath to wind up for the Conservative Opposition in a debate on the Labour Government's prices policy, she arrived at the despatch box with such a well-researched case that she was able to destroy the myth that the outgoing Conservative Government had left an £800-million deficit. … It is difficult to exaggerate either the extent to which research underpins her authority and power or the liking she has for statistics of any sort. Knowledge is power, and she loves retaining almost any sort of knowledge, although with something more than the lawyer's ability to read rapidly and retain facts for only as long as is necessary for a case."[31]

Frank Stanton's rise to the presidency of CBS was launched on a power base derived from the creation and presentation of factual detail about the market.[32] He started in CBS in 1935 as the head of a very small research unit. Stanton pioneered the idea of conducting surveys to find out who listened to which radio station, which programs they liked, and of discovering facts about the market and the competitive positions of the various stations. Much of Stanton's information was obtained from the *World Almanac*, which was potentially available to everyone:

> "Stanton had his tiny research department churning out facts and figures to salesmen trying to lure advertisers and choice affiliates from NBC. He was establishing himself as an executive with precise methods. ... Everyone called Stanton 'Doc.' ... Before long, his research was used in almost every facet of CBS's business – to help attract advertisers and audiences, to select and build programs, and to help coax affiliates to switch from NBC to CBS. By 1938, he was Research Director with a staff of one hundred."[33]

■ Tactic 7: Inspirational appeals

Yukl and Falbe identify emotion as the key factor in inspirational appeals.[34] The manager might make an emotional request, appeal to the target's values in order to generate enthusiasm. Equally, the manager might boost the target's confidence in being up to performing the required task. This tactic draws on the last of the *six principles of influence* – emotion.

Emotionally-charged and symbolic language will often be employed to bring out the importance of the task. Think of Kennedy's famous appeal: "Now the trumpet summons us again – not as a call to bear arms ... – but a call to bear the burden of a long twilight struggle year in and year out. ... And so, my fellow Americans: ask not what your country can do for you – ask what you can do for your country ..."[35]

As well as focusing on the target's sense of justice or loyalty, inspirational appeals may exploit the target's desire to achieve, excel, or win. Richard Branson's inspirational style of exercising influence is renowned for encouraging such loyalty from his staff that they were willing to accept modest wages in order for the

> As well as focusing on the target's sense of justice or loyalty, inspirational appeals may exploit the target's desire to achieve, excel, or win.

Virgin organization to succeed. Branson's enthusiasm, unkempt appearance and apparent indifference to material luxuries, the fact that his money went not on Savile Row suits or extravagant limousines, but back into the company, created a powerful role model for his staff and appealed to their sense of values and ideals. As Branson's biographer, Mick Brown, comments:

"Virgin had, to a large extent, been built on Branson's abilities at man-management and manipulation – his unrivalled capacity, as one friend put it, 'to get people to do things for him, and feel that they are the ones who have been done a favour.' Staff accepted lower wages because Virgin seemed to be a more agreeable place to work than anywhere else in the record industry. Life was not hidebound by rules or convention. The sense of hierarchy was so subtle as to be almost non-existent. No one spoke about 'management': it was simply Richard, Simon and Ken. Staff could feel, in that all-purpose adjective, 'involved.'"[36]

Branson was able to inspire people to excel and to have confidence in their ability to accomplish important and challenging tasks:

"[His] readiness to delegate responsibility and encourage people in tasks for which they had no particular qualification had been important in determining the mood of the company. By turning record-packers into talent scouts, magazine salesmen into managers, Branson had paid them the compliment of saying 'I trust you.' And that trust was invariably repaid with a fierce loyalty – if not always love – to Branson himself, and to the company."[37]

John Sculley influenced his targets through inspirational appeals when chairman and CEO of Apple Computers. Sculley successfully infused his Apple Macintosh factory manager, Debi Coleman, with such a strong vision of the future and with such a will to effect the changes which would realize that vision, that she encouraged workers to make the facility the best in the world.

Debi Coleman spoke of Sculley in visionary terms: "He and I can talk ideas for hours. When I walk into his office, it's like I become mesmerized by the future. ... It's a little like being in Star Wars. Like you're on the mother ship, guiding the federation."[38]

> **People are persuaded by reason, but moved by emotion.**

Language has a central role to play – it provides the inspiration and helps you to control the behavior of the other person to your advantage. Jack Welch at GE is masterful in his use of inspirational language which stresses the nature of business as a romantic, heroic enterprise with almost legendary qualities.

The power of inspirational influence stems from the fact that it taps into the target's emotions, and that it helps people feel good about what you want them to do. People are persuaded by reason, but moved by emotion. Given the choice of influence tactic, as Jeffrey Pfeffer argues, "Which would you choose: your heart or your head? I will pick the heart."[39]

As we discussed in chapter five, people are not computers: emotions and feelings are important parts of their choices and behavior. That is why tapping into the soft, informal side of a business, penetrating the shadow organization, is such an important part of the influential manager's tactical repertoire. As Pfeffer argues:

> "It's your head that sends you off to check Consumer Reports when you are thinking of purchasing a new car. It's your heart that buys the Jaguar, or the Porsche. It's your head that tells you that political campaign speeches cannot be believed or trusted, but it's your heart that responds to the best oratory, and makes you refuse to vote for people who come across as 'dull,' as though that were a reason to vote or not vote for a governmental representative."[40]

■ Tactic 8: Consultation

Yukl and Falbe describe the typical consultation tactic as when the influential manager seeks the target's participation in decision making and planning.[41] When a person is invited to help decide what to do and how to do it, that person is likely to identify with the decision and try to make it successful.

Consultation tactics activate principle two of the *six principles of influence* – the commitment process. The principle of psychological commitment suggests that we are bound to actions which we choose voluntarily without pressure; which, by being public, are difficult to change; and which make a statement to the outside world about us.

> Consulting people gets them involved. By discussing how to implement a proposal, targets become committed to its successful implementation. The targets' personal commitment represents an investment – once committed, they will not allow failure to happen.

Consulting people gets them involved. And by discussing how to implement a proposal, targets become committed to its successful implementation. The targets' personal commitment represents an investment – once committed, they will not allow failure to happen.

Lawrence A Bossidy, CEO of the $13 billion turnover company Allied Signal, has pursued a deliberate strategy of consultation to influence his employees to work with him in the corporate transformation:

> "In the first 60 days, I talked to probably 5,000 employees. I would go to Los Angeles and speak to 500 people, then to Phoenix and talk to another 500. I would stand on a loading dock and speak to people and answer their questions. We talked about what was wrong and what we should do about it. … I knew intuitively that I needed support at the bottom right from the outset. Go to the people. … I think it's important to try to get effective interaction with everybody in the company, to involve everyone.
>
> "It's something I continue to do. Besides talking to large groups, whenever I go to a location I host smaller, skip-level lunches, where I meet with groups of about 20 employees without name tags and without their bosses … we wanted to create an environment in which people will speak up …
>
> "People's mind-sets have changed. Employees are interested in our stock price now. You go into the lobbies where we've installed monitors, and people are tracking Allied Signal. Not just their sector but the whole company."[42]

Jack Stack, CEO of Springfield Remanufacturing Corporation, faced a decision which could have resulted in layoffs of 100 employees. After almost three months of trying to make the decision on his own, he held "town meetings" at all company sites and found that his employees were willing to work to bring on new products and ideas, rather than see fellow workers laid off. He commented later that the decision on the company's future had not been his to make as a manager; the decision had belonged to the employees.

Matching influence tactics to objectives and targets

Which of the eight weapons of influence are most effective? As Yukl and Falbe's research demonstrates, the simple answer is that no single influence tactic can be isolated as being superior to others.[43] As we discussed in chapter three (*Know Yourself*) and in chapter four (*Identify Your Target*), tactics must be chosen on the basis of the influence target and the influence objective sought.

Chapter three emphasized that to become influential, a manager must be sufficiently self-aware to think through what he or she wants to achieve – an identification of goals and objectives must precede any attempt to use influence.

In addition, the manager must be flexible in the means by which he pursues the attainment of that end-goal. He must match his behavioral style to suit the behavioral style of the target.

Yukl and Falbe have found that the range of influence objectives most commonly pursued by managers is as follows:

1. Ask the person to do a new task or work on a new project or account.

2. Ask the person to do a task faster or better.

3. Ask the person to change policies, plans, or procedures to accommodate your needs.

4. Ask the person to provide advice or help in solving a problem.

5. Ask the person to give or loan you additional resources such as funds, supplies, materials, or use of equipment, facilities, or personnel.

6. Ask the person to approve or sign off a proposal, product, report, or document.

7. Ask the person to support your proposals in a meeting with other managers or clients.

8. Ask for information needed to do your work.[44]

Influential managers must know which buttons to push with their potential allies, and which to avoid. This involves a thorough understanding of the target's values and needs. Not only must the manager match the impression which he projects to the target's self-image; he must also ensure that the stage and props match the image which he is presenting. This corresponds to our earlier discussion on Goffman's work in the field of impression management.

For example, a manager would need to know whether his target had a Thatcher-like desire to be approached with answers, rather than problems. If so, a tendency to start influence attempts with open-ended, exploratory problem solving could lead to rejection, despite good intentions.

The need for multiple influence tactics

Leading psychologists Bernard Keys and Thomas Case report that a combination of influence tactics are required for the really important influence attempts.[45] If you are trying to "sell" a major new strategy or complex project, it is not enough to rely on just one tactic to achieve your objective: you have no option but to use multiple influence tactics.

As Keys and Case argue:

"A successful attempt is likely to begin with homework to gather facts, a citation of parallel examples (who is doing this?), a marshalling of support of others ... precise timing and packaging of a presentation, and, in the case of initial resistance, persistence and repetition over weeks or even months. Less frequently, but sometimes successfully, managers may resort to manipulation, threats, or pulling rank."[46]

Lee Iococca used multiple influence tactics to achieve the turn-around at Chrysler, as Kotter describes:

"He developed a bold new vision of what Chrysler should be ... he (then) attracted, held onto, and elicited cooperation and teamwork from a large network ... labor leaders, a whole new management team, dealers, suppliers, some key government officials, and many others. He did so by articulating his agenda in emotionally powerful ways ('Remember, folks, we have a responsibility to save 600,000 jobs'), by using the credibility and relationships he had developed after a long and highly successful career in the automotive business, by communicating the new strategies in an intellectually powerful manner and in still other ways."[47]

Tactics for the boss, peers, and subordinates

Research by Yukl and Falbe shows that the type of tactics used by managers does not vary with the direction of the influence attempt, that is, whether it is horizontally across to peers, vertically up to superiors, or downward to subordinates.[48]

Four particular influence tactics are used more frequently than others, regardless of whether the target is a subordinate, peer, or superior:

- consultation,
- rational persuasion,
- inspirational appeals,
- ingratiation tactics.

It is the target and the objective, independent of the target's status relative to the influencer, which dictate the tactics used.

Softer or stronger strategic approaches?

The research shows that at all levels, softer strategies such as consultation, rational persuasion, inspirational appeals, ingratiation, and exchange tactics are the tactics of first choice for managers seeking to persuade people to cooperate with them.[49]

Stronger strategies, such as upward appeals and pressure tactics, are used when the target of influence is less likely to comply, especially if the target is a subordinate. In this case, a manager might resort to more traditional means for obtaining compliance.

Softer strategies pull people gently toward accepting your influence, whereas stronger strategies push people into accepting your influence.

It is the target and the objective, independent of the target's status relative to the influencer, which dictate the tactics used.

Jack Welch at GE is using soft strategies of influence to transform his organization and win in the 1990s. Traditionally, GE was the role model for the "whips and chains" approach to managing with a highly bureaucratic, vertical command and control structure.[50] Nowadays, however, Welch realizes that to succeed, "We've got to take out the boss element" and unleash the tremendous potential and energy of people, through turning to the "soft stuff," the skills of exercising influence. As Welch described in an interview with Noel Tichy and Ram Charan in the *Harvard Business Review*, "Above all else ... good leaders are open. They go up, down, and around their organization to reach people. ... It is all about human beings coming to see and accept things through a constant interactive process aimed at consensus."[51]

Anita Roddick, founder and managing director of Body Shop International, abhors formal/strong strategies for influencing her employees. Rather, she believes in soft approaches based around personal communication. This means that she visits stores to tell stories and listen to employees' concerns and holds regular meetings with cross-sections of employees, often at her home. She taps into the organization's informal networks. In addition, she encourages upward communication through a suggestion scheme irreverently named the "department of damned good ideas."[52]

Ingvar Kamprad, founder of IKEA, also advocates soft approaches to influence, and prefers to work through personal networks (using a "mouth-to-ear basis") rather than formal systems. He also seeds the organization with "culture bearers," individuals who exhibit management potential and share the company's values.[53]

Any manager contemplating which approach to use to influence others in the organization of the 1990s and beyond will always find the softer approaches much more effective than stronger ones.

Stronger approaches rely heavily on formal authority to be successful, and as Rosabeth Moss Kanter has written, the crutch of formal authority derived from hierarchical positions has disappeared in today's flat organizations.

However, it is not merely the disappearance of the power associated with formal position that has moved the softer approaches to center stage at the expense of the stronger approaches. It is also because individuals respond to different influence styles in psychologically different ways, making softer strategies invariably superior to stronger strategies.

Charles Handy argues that there are three different mechanisms for responding to the process of influence: (1) compliance, (2) identification, and (3) internalization.[54]

■ Compliance

Stronger approaches (such as pressure tactics, upward appeals, and rules) are normally used because the manager's power is sufficient to ensure that the influence attempt succeeds. This is the "whips and chains" approach which Jack Welch is striving to eliminate at GE. The target acknowledges that the manager has the power and grudgingly accepts it, precisely because the target has no other choice.

Compliance will always produce the desired outcome – the request is actioned, but not voluntarily. Compliance, therefore, has its limits – often an action which is imposed on an individual and carried out grudgingly would have been done freely, had the target been asked and had the target perceived that he or she had a choice in the matter.

Given our original definition of influence ("the skill to make others voluntarily change their attitudes to events, people and decisions so that your ideas are implemented"), obtaining compliance really limits your potential to use influence.

A further disadvantage of compliance lies in the fact that the target who has not complied voluntarily can abdicate responsibility when the chips are down – this is the "I was just obeying orders" syndrome. Remember the example of Marine Lieutenant Colonel Oliver North testifying during the Iran-Contra hearing that he would have jumped from a top-storey window, had his commander-in-chief so desired, and that he never once disobeyed orders. What North was also implying, of course, was that his behavior was all about compliance rather than positive choice or active agreement with what had been done.

Conversely, if the influence attempt is accepted freely, then the psychological adjustment mechanism will be either identification or internalization.

■ Identification

The recipient adopts the idea or proposal because he or she admires or identifies with the source or the initiator of influence, in a process similar to inspirational tactics. Identification works on inducing an emotional response, and as such, is diametrically opposed to compliance.

There are limits to this type of approach, however. It is difficult to maintain this type of emotional leadership over protracted periods of time. In addition, inspirational leaders will often be surrounded by followers who are just that – not initiators, but followers with a high degree of dependence upon the inspirational leader.

Look at the example of the inspirational South African leader, Nelson Mandela, who has inspired such a high level of identification among his followers that he has become almost indispensable, thus reducing the flexibility of his own party – the ANC – as a long-term stable organization. Similarly, the world-famous advertising agency Saatchi and Saatchi traded so heavily on the influential appeal of the Saatchi brothers, that the organization's flexibility to survive their acrimonious departure in 1995 was much reduced.

■ Internalization

This is the mechanism which most truly symbolizes the voluntary change which we wish to encourage in others so that they agree with, and buy into, the implementation of our ideas.

With the softer strategies which characterize internalization (such as consultation, rational persuasion, coalitions, and ingratiation), targets adopt your proposal as their own, because they internalize it as one of their possessions.

This is the approach Welch is pursuing at GE. He argues that there is no contradiction between his hard-nosed reputation for demanding superior performance and soft concepts like employee participation:

> "Welch and his lieutenants have selected three weapons, management techniques called Work-Out, Best Practices and Process Mapping. The first jimmies the locks that keep employees out of the decision-making process; the second seeks to smash the 'not invented here' syndrome and to spread good ideas quickly from one part of GE to another; the third is the tool the others most depend on. All foster

lots of employee involvement. Combined, they are designed to sustain the rapid growth in productivity that, Welch says, is the key to any corporation's survival in the competitive environment of the Nineties."[55]

To achieve internalization, pressure must not be exerted on individuals to accept influence. The targets must be totally free to argue about the influence and even to reject it. Acceptance must be entirely voluntary. Following a successful influence attempt, targets will believe that the ideas were their own, with no influence having been exerted upon them. If you are the manager who did successfully exert influence, such a denial of your role can be a bitter pill to swallow. But as we argued in chapter three, you must learn to play the backroom boy if you are to achieve true influence.

As Handy summarized it: "Internalization ... is the most lasting. Identification is the most pleasant. Compliance is the quickest."[56]

A typology of managerial influence

How do most current managers use influence – do they typically only use one or two strategies all the time, all eight or none at all?

The simple answer is that there are three types of managers who use different combinations. We will refer to these managerial types as "polymaths," "robots," and "hermits."

■ Polymaths

DEFINITION

Polymath managers use all eight tactics with above average frequency to influence others. They usually have a high need for achievement and may wish to implement a wide range of objectives. These are the archetypal managers who will use a multiplicity of tactics to achieve their goals, particularly when these goals are complex and critical.

Allied Signal's CEO, Lawrence A. Bossidy, is a typical polymath, who uses myriad different approaches to bring about changes in the company. Not only is Bossidy known as a straight-shooting, tough-minded, results-oriented business leader, he is also a charismatic and persistent coach, determined to help people learn and, in so doing, provide his company with the best prepared employees.

■ Robots

Robot managers are programmed to rely heavily on just one tactic – rational persuasion – to influence others. These are the archetypal, cerebral, expertise-oriented managers discussed in chapter one.

DEFINITION

While they may be reasonably successful in attempts to use influence which involve rational persuasion alone, when it comes to more complex attempts which require a range of tactics, their attempts are destined to fail.

Early on in his political career, Henry Kissinger identified the ineffectiveness of a purely rational approach when it came to the more complex and important influence attempts:

"Before I served as a consultant to Kennedy, I had believed, like most academics, that the process of decision-making was largely intellectual and all one had to do was to walk into the President's office and convince him of the correctness of one's view. This perspective I soon realized is as dangerously immature as it is widely held."[57]

■ Hermits

Although occupying a managerial role, hermit managers feel that they lack the power to influence anything. Because they feel so ineffectual, they almost resent the use of power and influence on the part of other members of the organization.

DEFINITION

The fact that they are so ineffectual means that they have no control over themselves or others around them – they are the organization's hermits.

The challenge for modern managers is to develop mastery over all eight tactics of influence, to become polymaths able to adopt a multiplicity of approaches to suit the environment and to achieve their objectives. Development of this polymath mastery is the subject of the next and final chapter.

CHAPTER SUMMARY

- This chapter has focussed on the need to develop a systematic approach to the exercise of influence which acknowledges the eight tactical weapons of influence open to the manager. These weapons are: (1) pressure, (2) upward appeals, (3) exchange, (4) coalitions, (5) ingratiation, (6) rational persuasion, (7) inspirational appeals, and (8) consultation.

- The chapter stressed the need to match the eight tactical weapons to your influence objectives and to your target's profile.

- The importance of using multiple tactics, particularly in more complex and important influence attempts, was highlighted, as was the range of tactics typically used when dealing with either superiors, peers, or subordinates.

- Tactics were then formulated into soft or strong strategic approaches. Soft influence strategies were presented as the approach of choice, not only because they suit the flat organizations of the 1990s, but also because they are more effective, tending as they do to deliver voluntary acceptance on the part of the person whom the manager is seeking to influence.

- Finally, we have also seen that the differing applications of influence tactics can be categorized into managerial types of sophisticated polymaths, single-track robots, and noninfluential hermits.

CONCEPT QUIZ

Do you understand the eight strategic weapons of influence and how to use them effectively?

1. Rational persuasion is the only acceptable way to influence people in business. *True or false?*

2. Ingratiation always works best regardless of your objective or the needs of your influence target. *True or false?*

3. A range of influence tactics should be used for the more important influence goals. *True or false?*

4. The most frequently used influence tactics are consultation, rational persuasion, inspirational appeals, and ingratiation. *True or false?*

5. Radically different influence tactics should be used when dealing with your superiors, peers, and subordinates. *True or false?*

6. The best way to get people to accept your attempts to influence them is always to start with a strong strategy, such as using pressure tactics, to show them who's boss. *True or false?*

7. Softer strategies of influence allow managers to get their targets to voluntarily change their minds. *True or false?*

8. Influence attempts based on one tactic – the preprogrammed robot approach – are always the most effective. *True or false?*

9. Being influential is all about keeping in with the boss – there is nothing else to it. *True or false?*

10. Just tell people what to do, and keep piling on the pressure – that's the way to really achieve the most influence. *True or false?*

Answers

1(F), 2(F), 3(T), 4(T), 5(F), 6(F), 7(T), 8(F), 9(F), 10(F).

MOVING FROM TASK TO PROCESS

Heartened by her success in persuading James that Butler was no longer up to the role, Laura was convinced that there was more to getting on in organizational life than just doing a good job.

Laura now realized that to be an effective manager, she had to be process- as well as task-oriented. In short, she became hooked on the idea of cultivating the skills of influence.

Laura thought she would try out her new agenda for managing. She set herself the objective of winning financial backing from global head-quarters to develop and market an entirely new product line in a market niche with huge potential.

She deliberated how she should approach the objective. Her natural choice of tactic led her to think about presenting a logical argument, supported by factual evidence – but she wondered whether this would work. The key decisionmaker was James: whatever James recommended to global headquarters, headquarters would automatically sanction. Yet Laura realized that James never responded to rational, numbers-driven analysis. Laura also understood that James disliked his people being seen to take the initiative. James was used to barking out orders and to having them obeyed. Laura thought that the key to getting what she wanted was to let James believe that investing in the new product range was James's own idea.

Laura decided to set up marketing and sales groups to examine the benefits of the proposed new product range. The groups became highly enthusiastic about the proposal, because it represented a new challenge for the sales people plus new earning possibilities, as well as promotions for those marketing staff chosen to manage it.

At the same time, Laura advised the external product development consultants to lobby James directly, as he was the key purseholder. She hinted that some corporate hospitality consistent with James's status might not go amiss as a foretaste to the business discussions proper.

Laura also suggested to James that he might like to spend some time with the sales and marketing teams. James agreed and when he subsequently met the teams, he mentioned that he had been assessing some new product ideas which could potentially benefit the company. The teams backed his proposal unequivocally and joked that James should twist Laura's arm to take the new project on board.

James returned to Laura's office and was proud to report the warm reception accorded to his new product proposal. "I want you to present a proposal for these new products when the American board visits the UK next week, Laura," said James, "Keep it short, go easy on the numbers, focus on top-line only. Got it?"

"Visionary idea, James," replied Laura, smiling to herself that there really was something to this influence business.

Review question

1. What did Laura do right this time?

SUMMARY CHECKLIST

❑ **Develop a systematic understanding of the tactics and strategies of influence.**

❑ **Match your influence tactics with your objectives and target.**

❑ **Use multiple influence tactics.**

❑ **Always start with softer influence strategies rather than strong.**

ACTION CHECKLIST

1. Review how you currently attempt to secure agreement to a proposal from a third party.

_____

_____

2. Reflect on whether the influence goal determines the choice of tactics you use.

_____

_____

3. Identify how the target may affect your choice of tactics and why.

_____

_____

4. Think of a time when you have been unsuccessful in an attempt to influence someone, and list the reasons for your failure. What have you learned?

_____

_____

5. Choose a reasonably important influence goal. Identify the target(s), and try to map out the multiplicity of tactics that you might use to get your way.

_____

_____

6. Once you have selected your tactics, evaluate the criteria you have used to select tactics. Are these correct and appropriate, in view of what you are trying to achieve and the needs of your target?

_____

_____

7. Implement your strategy.

_____

_____

8. Review your success – what did you do right and what did you do wrong?

_____

_____

9. Select another influence goal.

_____

_____

10. Repeat the above process.

_____

_____

11. Review, and keep practicing!

_____

_____

chapter seven

THE ROAD TO MASTERY

- Self-assessment exercise
- The key steps to becoming an influential manager: a summary
- Managing the learning process
- Developing into a master in the use of influence
- "Stomaching the struggle:" developing the will to exert influence
- Chapter summary
- Concept quiz
- Feature case study
- Summary checklist
- Action checklist

This chapter summarizes why influence needs to be re-invented for the new world of work and what the key steps are to becoming an influential manager.

It examines the four interrelated steps which managers must undertake to develop the skills of influence. It shows how managers can systematically control the skills development process.

The various stages in developing mastery in the skills of influence are discussed: these are the novice, advanced beginner, competent, proficient, and expert stages. This classification alerts managers to the various developmental processes they will go through and, by explaining the issues in play, it builds self-confidence.

The chapter finally focuses on developing the will to exercise influence – aspiring managers must passionately want to take charge of their lives if they wish to become truly influential and get things done in their organizations.

SELF-ASSESSMENT EXERCISE

Reexamining your profile – are you using influence effectively?

The aim of this exercise is to revisit the first self-assessment exercise completed in chapter one and assess whether your reading of this book has modified your behavior in the area of influencing others.

1. List all those people you work with or through.

_____

_____

_____

2. List the people in the organization who may be useful to know.

_____

_____

_____

3. List the major tasks you do at work.

_____

_____

_____

4. Estimate the proportion of time you spend between the following:
   (a) building relationships,
   (b) completing your major tasks,
   (c) attending formal meetings.

_____

_____

_____

5. What are the main problems you encounter in seeking to influence others at work?

_____

_____

_____

Follow-up

Compare the results you produced now with those when you initially completed this exercise.

- How have you changed?
- How differently do you now see things?
- Has the nature of your existing relationships changed? If so, in what way, and why?
- Has your network of contacts increased?
- Has the proportion of time you spend in building relationships increased or remained the same?
- Are you still primarily task-driven?
- Have the problems you encountered in seeking to influence others at work changed? If "yes," analyze why the problems have changed and what you have learnt to do differently.
- What are the remaining problems of influencing others that you now need to work on?
- What steps do you intend to take to develop new skills?

If some changes have started to take place, then it is likely that you are already on the way to taking control of yourself and developing the skills of influence. You are now ready to embark on the challenge of systematically developing the skills which will allow you to use influence to get things done.

The key steps to becoming an influential manager: a summary

We started in chapter one by examining the relationship between influence skills and managerial effectiveness. We looked at the changing nature of organizations in the 1990s and the subsequent impact on the nature of the manager's role. The changing macroenvironment, technological progress, the increasing diversity of the values and goals of employees and the move toward flatter, interdependent organizations, all served to dramatically reduce the effectiveness of formal authority. As a result, influence skills have become central to the repertoire of techniques and strategies needed by managers to achieve things.

Chapter two focussed on developing an understanding of the process of influence. The complex relationship between power and influence was discussed. We identified the *seven power levers* open to all managers: (1) resources, (2) information, (3) expertise, (4) connections, (5) coercion, (6) position, and (7) personal power. The *six principles of influence* through which managers can activate power were also outlined: (1) contrast, (2) historical commitments and consistency, (3) scarcity, (4) social proof, (5) liking and ingratiation, and (6) emotion.

We saw that successful application of the principles of influence allows managers to activate power and get things done in the interdependent organizations of the 1990s.

Following on from the examination of why managers need to reinvent the skills of influence, and what these skills were, we then presented the *four key steps to becoming an influential manager*:

Step one - know yourself focussed on the need for self-understanding before a manager can influence effectively. Beliefs, values, and assumptions all have an impact on a manager's success in influencing others for acceptance of his goals.

The need for the conscious management of beliefs, values, and assumptions was stressed - this allows a manager to control and manipulate the range of impressions he makes on the people he needs to influence.

The chapter highlighted the importance of identifying goals clearly and of separating emotions from business objectives. It demonstrated why a manager must be flexible in how he ultimately attains his goal and why sometimes a manager's ego should take a back seat for the sake of longer-term goals. This section also showed that becoming influential requires tremendous energy, physical stamina, and mental perseverance.

Step two - identify your target moved from understanding yourself to a thorough analysis of your target. You must learn to establish who is important in getting your goal accomplished and to correctly judge the kinds of behavior, values, attitudes, and ideas which your influence target can accept. This places you firmly in control of the influence process.

A manager's awareness of how he perceives people can prevent the routine errors of interpretation which the chapter identifies. Accurate perception management requires a manager to draw upon multiple indicators, such as verbal and nonverbal cues, organizational factors, and personal issues. So-called common sense judgments, which may mislead, should be avoided.

Step three - diagnose the system explained the relationship between the hidden system of the organization and successful influencing behavior. The hidden system was shown to be a stronger determinant of what types of behavior were deemed to be acceptable than the "proper," formal channels of authority.

The culture and networks of organizations were shown to be the prime components of this hidden system. We saw how culture serves as an unwritten guide to the kinds of influencing behavior which the organization is willing to accept. Human networks were shown to be the channels through which we use the information which we have gathered to actively work the informal system.

Step four - decide on strategy and tactics explained the strategy and tactics of influence. There are *eight key tactics of influence*: (1) pressure tactics, (2) upward appeals, (3) rational appeals, (4) exchange tactics, (5) coalition tactics, (6) ingratiation tactics, (7) inspirational appeals, and (8) consultation tactics.

> It is one thing to understand the steps to becoming an influential manager ... and quite another thing to actually do it, but do it you must because managing with influence is essential for those who seek to get things accomplished.

The chapter underlined the need to always match influence tactics with influence objectives and the profile of the target of influence. It is equally important to employ a multiplicity of tactics to achieve the more important attempts to influence others.

Strategies fall into either soft or strong approaches to getting people to agree. Soft influence strategies are usually the preferred choice in the flat, interdependent organizations of the 1990s.

We also saw that the ways that managers apply influence tactics can be typified into three groups: the sophisticated polymath manager (able to deploy a wide variety of tactics), the mediocre robot manager (programmed to execute a very limited number of tactics), and the organizational hermit (a conscientious objector to the whole world of influence who has opted out of any attempt whatsoever to become influential).

It is one thing to understand the steps to becoming an influential manager - why you need influence; what it is; how to diagnose it; what its sources are; what strategies and tactics you should employ to use it – it is quite another thing to actually do it. But do it you must, because managing with influence is essential for those who seek to get things accomplished. Nothing happens in organizations or in life in the 1990s if you lack the skills to use influence effectively. Authority is out; influence is in. As James Goldsmith's old friend Arnaud de Borchgrave, now editor of the *Washington Times*, puts it: "Jimmy is not interested in power. He is a man who is interested in influence, which is quite different."[1]

Implementing the skills of influence may well involve conflict, risks, and errors. Overcoming these obstacles requires the will to succeed and the ability to cope with a fight. As a leading Harvard academic comments:

"It is easy and often comfortable to feel powerless - to say, 'I don't know what to do, I don't have the power to get it done, and besides, I can't really stomach the struggle that may be involved.' It is easy, and now quite common, to say, when confronted with some mistake in your organization, 'It's not really my responsibility, I can't do anything about it anyway, and if the company wants to do that, well, that's why the senior executives get the big money - it's their responsibility.'"[2]

> Implementing the skills of influence may well involve conflict, risks, and errors.

Managing the learning process

Chapter six included a systematic evaluation of the *eight tactics of influence*. To transform that systematic evaluation into real-life action, it is necessary to follow a particular cycle of learning, a behavioral model which can be applied to a wide range of situations in everyday life.

This model entails four interrelated learning stages:[3]

1. Understand what influence is, not only as an idea, but what it means in practice.
2. Practice exercising influence.
3. Encourage feedback on your influencing performance.
4. Use the skills so frequently that they become part of your natural behavior.

■ Stage 1: Gain understanding

You have already achieved this stage because the material presented in this book has provided you with an understanding of what influence is, not only as an idea, but what it means in practice.

- Each chapter began with a self-assessment exercise designed to help you to evaluate how much you already knew about the skills of influence.

- The material following each self-assessment exercise helped you to understand the concepts underpinning the skills. The concept quiz allowed you to check your understanding of these concepts.

> You have already achieved stage one because the material presented in this book has provided you with an understanding of what influence is, not only as an idea, but what it means in practice.

- The feature case study then provided insights into some of the behavioral issues which others have had to confront when putting the skills of influence into practice.

- The summary checklist, derived from the skills concepts, then identified the specific forms of behavior that a manager needs to acquire.

- Finally, the action checklist presented examples of opportunities that managers might use when they finally set out to use the skills of influence.

Your challenge now is to complete stages two, three and four.

■ Stage 2: Practice using influence

You must seek out every opportunity to practice using influence in everyday life.

■ Stage 3: Feedback

Having understood the theoretical concepts and applied them to concrete situations, you must now review how well you applied them – by standing back from the situation and objectively assessing what happened, what succeeded, and what failed.

As part of this evaluation process, you may well wish to revisit many of the self-assessment exercises, action checklists, and episodes of the feature case study presented in the book. The scoring systems, review questions, and summary checklists all provide a ready-made toolkit to assess your development.

You should also accept feedback on your performance from others, and then draw general principles from your successes and failures - what have I learnt, how can I apply it? The skill is to learn from these concrete experiences, modify your ideas appropriately, apply them to new situations – and then repeat the whole cycle again. There is a continuous learning loop between stages two and three.

■ Stage 4: Integration into the repertoire

You must use the skills sufficiently often so that through constant modification and practice, the skills enter your standard behavioral repertoire.

> The skill is to learn from these concrete experiences, modify your ideas appropriately, apply them to new situations – and then repeat the whole cycle again.

The process of moving from step one through to step four (to be able to apply the skills of influence successfully) is a long one, and not something that can be achieved overnight. The task will be greatly simplified by knowing how to manage the learning process, a topic discussed below.

Developing into a master in the use of influence

You will inevitably pass a number of clearly defined milestones as you increase your competence. The aspiring influential manager will inevitably pass through the milestones of (1) novice, (2) advanced beginner, (3) competence, and then (4) proficiency, before achieving (5) expertise.[4] Knowing where these milestones are can provide reassurance and allow you to retain self-confidence, particularly in the early parts of your journey when you are likely to succeed in some situations, but fail or make mistakes in others.

■ Milestone 1: The novice

As a novice, the manager will learn the rules of influence. More often than not, he or she will follow them slavishly. This book has outlined what these basic rules are. At this stage, the manager will probably be highly cerebral and analytical in his or her approach to influence, and expect that definite rules and procedures produce set results.

However, having developed a conceptual understanding of the uses of influence, the challenge is then to leave the first milestone behind and start to put the new understanding into practice.

■ Milestone 2: The advanced beginner

This is where the manager starts to practice using the rules of influence in real situations. His experience will help him to develop an understanding of the process of influence which reaches into the hidden, shadowy system of the organization, the world of culture, networks, norms, and values.

Remember how in chapter five, Laura recalled learning during her MBA course something about "moles" and "mouths," but thought that it sounded like something out of a novel until she applied it to her own life situation? Once Laura had applied the concepts, she began to recognize certain patterns and discover the unstated norms, rules, and culture surrounding her job, which up to then she just had not noticed.

> At the second milestone the manager starts to practice using the rules of influence in real situations.

■ Milestone 3: Competence

A virtuous circle begins to develop, as the manager experiments with more complex tactics and draws on an increasingly wide set of cues. The manager will start to do things by feel, rather than by rote. His confidence level will increase, and allow him to take conscious risks.

Some influence attempts fail. Some succeed. You learn from both outcomes. The key thing is make the attempt. In our case study, for example, Laura took a calculated risk in her attempt to convince James to launch the new product range; she consciously planned the process in her discussions with the supportive Neil; she then tried a range of new behaviors; she experimented with a multiplicity of influence tactics, and she was successful.

■ Milestone 4: Proficiency

At milestone three, there was still a certain amount of trial and error, with conscious, rational planning preceding the influence attempt.

Once proficiency is reached, conscious planning is entirely replaced by unconscious awareness. Like someone learning how to drive who realizes that there is no need to continually look at the pedals and the gear stick when changing gear, the manager will now be able to act continually by feel. The range of techniques available to him is now complete.

He will begin to see the potential influence goal holistically and move toward the insightful and intuitive understanding of the situation as described by Mintzberg. This is the type of perception at which the more streetwise manager described in chapter one is naturally skilled. At the same time, the automatic use of multiple influence tactics begins to emerge.

John Sculley of Pepsico and Apple Computers is proficient, perhaps even expert, in his application of influence skills. Consider the proficiency with which he handled the process through which he was recruited to Apple Computers by Steve Jobs and his hired headhunter, Gerald Roche, in 1982:[5]

"Jobs and Markkula flew to New York to meet him [Sculley] in December, but he was cool during the meeting and afterwards told Roche he wasn't interested. That didn't deter Roche. ... It left Jobs absolutely intrigued. ... In January they showed him Lisa [the new Apple III PC] and went out to dinner at the Four Seasons. In early March ... Jobs persuaded him to stop in Cupertino. ... There were a number of reasons why Jobs wanted Sculley so much ... as time went on, Jobs simply got caught up in the challenge of luring him to Apple and converting him to Apple's cause. Jobs ... had so much money it was embarrassing. Nothing made him salivate like the thing he couldn't get."[6]

Through his unconscious, intuitive and skillful use of the scarcity principle, of timing and delay tactics, and through his manipulation of Job's escalating commitment, Sculley effortlessly lured Jobs toward him. It was the same intuitive skills which were to allow Sculley eventually to force Jobs out of the company.

■ Milestone 5: Expert

Once a manager has passed this milestone, the journey on the road to mastery in the use of influence is complete - and he will have emerged as a naturally insightful/intuitive influencer, to use Mintzberg's term. The manager will no longer apply rules mechanistically, but will instead use feeling and intuition for a complete understanding of situations. The intuitively influential manager "just knows" what to do.

Such expert managers successfully handle the ambiguity, inconsistency, and chaos naturally found in organizational life in an effortless fashion. This is the stage that GE's Jack Welch has reached - he has such an intuitive feel for the processes he wishes to use to alter people's behavior that one of the major change processes - "Work-out" - for example, was conceived during a spontaneous debate during a helicopter journey in 1988 to GE's headquarters in Connecticut.[7]

"Stomaching the struggle"
Developing the will to exert influence

Using influence successfully means more than a simple application of theoretical concepts. A manager needs to have the will to "stomach the struggle" which successful attempts to use influence inevitably involve.

In our case study, Laura switched from total reliance on

the cerebral/expertise-based approach toward more intuitive/ process-oriented skills of influence. This switch led her to successfully identify strategies and tactics to handle the people and situations which she confronted, and to reach the goals she sought to achieve.

What really marks Laura out is that she had the will and personal courage to change. How much easier it would have been to have sat back and refused to accept the challenge to change and develop, in favor of the quiet life of the ineffective hermit. Instead, Laura had the motivation and conviction to want to exercise influence so that she could make things happen in her organization.

A manager who aspires to be influential will need to develop the type of grim determination demonstrated by Laura, but he will have some major advantages over Laura in embarking on the process of change. In the first place, he will have read this book and so will possess a framework to understand the psychological processes strategy, and tactics necessary for performing in an area which does not come naturally.

Secondly, he should now have self-confidence and specific competences gained from the self-assessment exercises and the case study. He should continue to develop these skills in a virtuous circle of action, feedback, and modified action.

Thirdly, he will have the skills framework to consciously manage the process of continuous learning and to monitor his progress toward the various development milestones.

All he will need on top of that is the will to develop, which Laura demonstrated in such abundance. As Margaret Thatcher's father, Alderman Roberts, was so fond of saying to her:

> "It is easy to be a starter,
> But are you a sticker too?
> It is easy enough to begin a job,
> It is harder to see it through."[8]

Many managers find the example of Alderman Roberts and of

Laura hard to follow - they find following through on the change process difficult. Typical excuses which they make for themselves include:

- "That's sounds fine for someone else, but it's not really appropriate for me."
- "I'm no good at these touchy-feely things, I would rather deal in concrete facts and figures."
- "I have never been any good at working with people; you have to be born with that skill."
- "I really can't spare the time or effort to develop these skills, I've got so much work to do."

Becoming influential requires a manager to take charge of himself and his learning, and to stop making excuses. It requires the ability to develop what Charles Handy calls a "proper selfishness," that is, a sense of responsibility for himself and sufficient self-confidence to believe that he can get what he wants in life.[9] Individuals who have enough courage and "proper selfishness" will take charge of themselves and overcome the discomforts that will inevitably come.

> Many managers find following through on the change process difficult.

This book has provided you with the ideas and tools. It is now up to you as an individual to accept the challenge of becoming an influential member of your organization.

The challenge ahead is best evoked by President John F. Kennedy's inaugural address on Friday, January 20, 1961: "Let us begin. In your hands, my fellow citizens, more than mine, will rest the success or failure of our course."[10]

CHAPTER SUMMARY

- This chapter has summarized the critical need to reinvent influence in the new world of work. It has outlined the steps involved in becoming an influential manager.

- It has shown that to develop the skills of influence, the manager must pass through *four learning stages*: (1) understanding the skills; (2) implementing the skills; (3) feedback, leading to implementation of ideas modified by this feedback; and (4) integration of the successfully modified skills into an extensive, intuitive repertoire.

- It describes the *five development milestones*, from novice right through to expert. This insight aids confidence building and allows managers to accurately gauge their progress toward the milestone of mastery in the use of influence.

- The chapter ended by emphasizing that the expert influencer must develop a "proper selfishness" coupled with the will both to influence and to overcome the discomforts which will inevitably arise.

- Authority is out. Influence is in.

- Developing mastery in the exercise of influence is the key management challenge in the new world of work.

CONCEPT QUIZ

Do you understand the road to mastery and how to put the skills of influence into operation?

1. Influence has replaced authority as the key skill in the new world of work. *True or false?*

2. You cannot learn how to influence others: you either have it or you don't. *True or false?*

3. There are no models of learning which can help a manager to develop the skills of influence. *True or false?*

4. Developing a skill takes time and managers pass a variety of milestones in developing mastery in the use of influence. *True or false?*

5. A skill is a system of behavior that can be applied in a wide range of circumstances. *True or false?*

6. The four steps to becoming an influential manager are: know yourself; identify your target; diagnose the system; and understand strategy and tactics. *True or false?*

7. Developing the skills of influence requires you to have the will to change and take control of your life. *True or false?*

8. Change invariably involves both pleasure and pain. *True or false?*

9. Influence in the new world of work empowers the manager to get things done. *True or false?*

10. I am going to change and develop the skills for using influence. *True or false?*

Answers

1(T), 2(F), 3(F), 4(T), 5(T), 6(T), 7(T), 8(T), 9(T), 10(T).

PROFICIENCY AND PROMOTION

The managing director smiled as she inspected the assembly line producing the new range. Launched ahead of schedule, the new range was already generating significant additional profit for the company.

She paused briefly to discuss with the new quality and customer care manager the zero rejects campaign and the results of the six-monthly business review held with the top customer whose business Laura had not only successfully retained, but had also increased.

So much had happened since James had suddenly left the group to spend more time messing around in boats and Laura had been promoted to managing director.

Laura shuddered when she remembered the appalling tactical errors she had made as a novice when she had first become marketing director: such as telling James outright that she wanted his job; highlighting the disastrous product launch initiated just before Laura had joined the company; bluntly telling James why one of his protégés should be dismissed. ...

Laura comforted herself with the thought that at least she had learned from her experiences and had become reasonably proficient in using influence. She smiled when she thought how she had won unthinking support from Mike Stamper for her research proposal simply by appealing to his vanity; how she had allowed James to "own" her idea for the new product range; how she had leaked information into the informal network to achieve the departure of Butler. ...

She also recognized the help which Neil had brought her by offering her continual feedback on her performance and by helping her to plan. Getting this far had not been easy. Laura thought of the endless 70-hour weeks, the conflicts at work, the pressure on family and social life which both she and Neil had had to endure. But it had been worth it - she was now in control of herself and of her life. Laura hurried on - she had to conduct the appraisal of one of her senior managers in a couple of minutes.

As Laura entered the meeting room, she saw the manager close a paperback entitled *Reinventing Influence* and replace it in his briefcase. The appraisal went well; Laura finally asked the appraisee where he saw his career objectives five years hence - "Oh, I'm just a backroom boy," he replied, "much too busy crunching the numbers to think about things like that." Laura smiled ruefully: if only she had had the benefit of *Reinventing Influence* when she had first set foot on the road to mastering influence. ...

SUMMARY CHECKLIST

❑ **Know and understand yourself.**

❑ **Identify your target.**

❑ **Diagnose the system.**

❑ **Decide on your strategy and tactics.**

❑ **Practice.**

❑ **Review.**

❑ **Modify ideas in light of review and feedback.**

❑ **Practice and test out again.**

ACTION CHECKLIST

1. Reread all the chapter summaries of this book so that you understand what influence is, both conceptually and behaviorally.

_____

_____

2. Discuss your skills with people who will be honest.

_____

_____

3. Identify a personal action plan for the various skills you wish to develop.

_____

_____

4. Keep a log to help you monitor your progress.

_____

_____

5. Practice - always start with a reasonably safe learning situation such as a nonwork-related goal, and only then progress to more complex situations.

_____

_____

6. Evaluate yourself - be honest.

_____

_____

7. Ask for other people's evaluations of your performance.

_____

_____

8. Develop learning points from your experiences.

_____

_____

9. Try them out again.

_____

_____

10. And continue to repeat the cycle.

_____

_____

notes

chapter one

1. Mintzberg, H. (1990) "The Manager's Job: Folklore and Fact" in J. Gabarro (ed.) *Managing People and Organizations* (Boston, MA: Harvard Business School Publications, 1992) pp 13–32. Reprinted by permission of Harvard Business Review. Copyright © 1990 by the President and Fellows of Harvard College, all rights reserved.
2. Oncken, W. Jr. & Wass, D.L (1974) "Management Time: Who's Got the Monkey?" in J. Gabarro (ed.), ibid., pp 50–56.
3. Mintzberg, "The Manager's Job: Folklore and Fact," pp 14–18.
4. Mintzberg, ibid., p 30.
5. Mintzberg, H., *Mintzberg on Management: Inside Our Strange World of Organizations* (New York: The Free Press, 1989) pp 48–55.
6. Mintzberg, "The Manager's Job: Folklore and Fact," p 30.
7. Davies, D. "Professional Promiscuity," *The Times Higher Educational Supplement*, 30 April 1993, p 24.
8. Bradley, I.C. *Enlightened Entrepreneurs* (Avon: Bath Press, 1987).
9. Machiavelli, N., *The Prince* (London: Penguin Books, 1970).
10. Pettigrew, A. "Information as a Power Resource," *Sociology*, 6ii, (1972) pp 187–204.
11. Bennett, A. "Going Global: The Chief Executive in the Year 2000 Will be Experienced Abroad," *Wall Street Journal*, 27 Feb. 1989, p 3. Reprinted by permission of *Wall Street Journal* © 1989, Dow Jones & Company, Inc. All rights reserved worldwide.
12. Bessant, J. *Managing Advanced Manufacturing Technology* (Oxford, NCC/Blackwell, 1991), p. 57.
13. Leavitt, H.J. & Whisler, T.L. "Management in the 1980s," *Harvard Business Review*, Nov./Dec. 1958, pp 41–48.
14. Coates, J. in Sanderson, S.R. & Schein, L. "Sizing Up the Down-Sizing Era," *Across the Board: The Conference Board Magazine*, 23, No.11, Nov. 1986, p 15.
15. Green, C. "Middle Managers Are Still Sitting Ducks," *Business Week*, 16 Sept. 1985, p 34.

16. Kanter, R.M. *When Giants Learn To Dance* (London: Unwin Hyman, 1989) p 361. Reprinted with the permission of Simon and Schuster from *When Giants Learn to Dance* by Rosabeth Moss Kanter. Copyright © by Rosabeth Moss Kanter.

17. Ibid., p 152.

18. Ibid., pp 153–154.

19. Harrison, B. & Bluestone, B. *The Great U-turn* (New York: Basic Books, 1988) pp 3–20.

20. Gates, B. *The Road Ahead* (London: Viking, Penguin Books, 1995) p 31.

21. Kanter, *When Giants Learn To Dance*, p 129.

22. Peters, T. & Austen, N. *A Passion For Excellence* (London: Fontana, 1989).

23. Reich, R.B. "Who Is Them?," *Harvard Business Review*, Jan.–Feb. 1990, p 62. Reprinted by permission of Harvard Business Review. Copyright © 1990 by the President and Fellows of Harvard College, all rights reserved.

24. Ibid., p 64.

25. Ibid., p 63.

26. Drucker, P. *The New Realities* (London: Heinemann Professional Publishing, Mandarin Paperback, 1990).

27. Reich, "Who Is Them?," p 63.

28. Ibid., p 65.

29. Bennett, "Going Global: The Chief Executive in the Year 2000 Will be Experienced Abroad," p 1.

30. Ibid., p 4.

31. Ibid., p 5.

32. Department of Education and Employment unpublished estimate: April 1996.

33. Handy, C. *The Empty Raincoat* (London: Hutchinson, 1994) p 73.

34. Stewart, T.A. "GE Keeps Those Ideas Coming," *Fortune*, 12 Aug. 1991, p 24. Reprinted with the permission of Fortune Magazine, © 1991.

35. Kanter, *When Giants Learn To Dance*, p 92.

36. Ibid., p 361.

37. Toffler, A. *Future Shock* (London: Pan, 1970).

38. Miles, R.E. "Adapting to Technology and Competition: A New Industrial Relations System for the 21st Century," *California Management Review*, Winter 1989, pp 9–28.

39. Coulsdon-Thomas, C. & Coe, T. *The Flat Organisation: Philosophy and Practice* (Corby: British Institute of Management, 1991) pp 10–11.

chapter two

1. Pfeffer, J. *Managing With Power: Politics and Influence in Organizations* (Boston, MA: Harvard Business School Press, 1992) pp 83–92. Reprinted by permission of Harvard Business School Press. Copyright © 1992 by the President and Fellows of Harvard College, all rights reserved.
2. Kearns, D. "Lyndon Johnson and the American Dream," *The Atlantic Monthly*, May 1976, p 41.
3. Jennings, R., Cox, C. & Cooper, C.L. *Business Elites: The Pyschology of the Entrepreneurs and Intrapreneurs* (London: Routledge, 1994) p 19. Reprinted with permission of International Thomson Publishing Services.
4. Ibid., p 19.
5. Ibid., p 77.
6. Ibid., p 79.
7. Ibid., p 77.
8. Meyer, H.E. "Shootout at the Johns-Manville Corral," *Fortune*, Oct. 1976, pp 146–154. Reprinted with permission of Fortune Magazine © 1976.
9. Kakabadse, A., Ludlow, R. & Vinnicombe, S. *Working in Organisations* (London: Penguin, 1988) p 216.
10. Stewart, T.A. "GE Keeps Those Ideas Coming," *Fortune*, 12 Aug. 1991, p 24.
11. Chippindale, P. & Horrie, C. *Stick It Up Your Punter: The Rise and Fall of the Sun* (London: William Heinemann Ltd, 1990) pp 328–329. Reprinted by permission of the Peters Fraser and Dunlop Group Ltd and Reed International Books.
12. Pfeffer, *Managing With Power: Politics and Influence in Organizations*, pp 187-188.
13. Cialdini, R.B. *Influence: Science and Practice* (Glenview, IL: Scott, Foresman and Company, 1985) pp 12–13. Reprinted by permission of Addison-Wesley Educational Publishers Inc..
14. Ibid., p 12.
15. Ibid., pp 13–14.

16. Pfeffer, *Managing With Power: Politics and Influence in Organizations*, pp 191-192.

17. Cialdini, *Influence: Science and Practice*, p 52.

18. Ibid., p 52.

19. Gardner, J.W. *On Leadership* (New York: Free Press, 1990).

20. Salancik, G.R. "Commitment and Control of Organizational Behavior and Belief," *New Directions in Organizational Behavior*, edited by Straw, B.M. & Salancik, G.R. (Chicago: St Clair Press, 1977) pp 1–54.

21. Pfeffer, *Managing With Power: Politics and Influence in Organizations*, pp 194–195.

22. Cialdini, *Influence: Science and Practice*, pp 200–201.

23. Pfeffer, *Managing With Power: Politics and Influence in Organizations*, pp 201–203.

24. Brehm, J.W. *A Theory of Psychological Reactance* (New York: Academic Press, 1966).

25. Cialdini, *Influence: Science and Practice*, p 201.

26. Pfeffer, *Managing With Power: Politics and Influence in Organizations*, p 203.

27. Cialdini, *Influence: Science and Practice*, p 98.

28. Gandossy, R.P. *Bad Business: The OPM Scandal and the Seduction of the Establishment* (New York: Basic Books, 1985) pp 12–13.

29. Pfeffer, *Managing With Power: Politics and Influence in Organizations*, p 208.

30. Berscheid, E. & Hatfield Walster, E. *Interpersonal Attraction* (Reading, MA: Addison-Wesley, 1969).

31. Pfeffer, *Managing With Power: Politics and Influence in Organizations*, p 208.

32. Festinger, L. "A Theory of Social Comparison Processes," *Human Relations*, 7 (1954), pp 117–140.

33. Pfeffer, *Managing With Power: Politics and Influence in Organizations*, pp 212-213.

34. Cialdini, *Influence: Science and Practice*, pp 140–172.

35. Byrne, D. *The Attraction Paradigm* (New York: Academic Press, 1971).

36. Adams, G.R. "Physical Attractiveness Research: Towards a Developmental Social Psychology of Beauty," *Human Development*, 20 (1977), pp 217–239.

37. Ross J. & Ferris, K.R. "Interpersonal Attraction and Organisational

Outcomes: A Field Examination," *Administrative Science Quarterly*, 26 (1981), pp 617–632.

38. Berscheid, E. & Hatfield Walster, E. *Interpersonal Attraction* (Reading, MA: Addison Wesley, 1969).

39. Sherif, M. *et al.*, *Intergroup Conflict and Cooperation: The Robbers' Cave Experiment* (University of Oklahoma Institute of Intergroup Relations, 1961).

40. Manis, M., Cornell, S.D. & Moore, J.C. "Transmission of Attitude-Relevant Information Through a Communication Chain," *Journal Of Personality and Social Psychology*, 30 (1974), pp 81–94.

41. Pfeffer, *Managing With Power: Politics and Influence in Organizations*, p 220.

42. Ibid., p 221.

43. Hochschild, A. *The Managed Heart* (Berkeley: University of California Press, 1983).

44. Rafaeli, A., & Sutton, R.I. "The Expression Of Emotion in Organizational Life," *Research in Organizational Behavior*, edited by Staw, B.M., Vol. 11, Greenwich, CT: JAI Press, 1989) pp 15–16.

45. Tidd, K.L. & Lockard, J.S. "Monetary Significance of the Affiliative Smile," *Bulletin of the Psychonomic Society*, 11 (1978), pp 344–346.

chapter three

1. Simmons, J. "Reeducation of a Company Man," *Business Week*, Oct. 1989, p 78. Reprinted by permission of Business Week.

2. Goffman, E. *The Presentation of Self in Everyday Life* (London: Penguin Books, 1978). Reprinted by permission of Allen Lane The Penguin Press, 1969 and Doubleday, copyright © Erving Goffman, 1959.

3. Ibid., p 25.

4. Ibid., p 26.

5. Ibid., p 27.

6. Thomson, A. *Margaret Thatcher: The Woman Within* (London: W.H. Allen, 1989) p 222. Reprinted by permission of the Sharland Organisation and the author Andrew Thomson.

7. Ibid., pp 222–223.

8. Gardner, W.L. & Martinko, M.J. "Impression Management: An Observational Study Linking Audience Characteristics with Verbal Self-Presentation," *Academy of Management Journal*, 31 (1988), pp 42–65.

9. Tichy, N.M. & Charan, R. "The CEO as Coach: An Interview with Allied Signal's Lawrence A. Bossidy," *Harvard Business Review*, March–April 1995, p 76. Reprinted by permission of Harvard Business Review. Copyright © 1995 by the President and Fellows of Harvard College, all rights reserved.

10. Swann, W.B. & Ely, R.J. "A Battle of Wills: Self-Verification Versus Behavioural Confirmation", *Journal of Personality and Social Psychology*, 46 (1984), pp 1287–1302.

11. Thomson, *Margaret Thatcher: The Woman Within*, p 220.

12. Ibid., p 219.

13. Ibid., p 222.

14. Ibid., p 224.

15. Brown, M. *Richard Branson: The Inside Story* (London: Headline Book Publishing, 1994) pp 213–215. Reprinted by permission of The Peters Fraser & Dunlop Group Ltd.

16. Ibid., pp 213–214.

17. Ibid., pp 290–291, comment on photograph 38.

18. Torbert, W.R. *Managing the Corporate Dream: Restructuring for Long-Term Success* (Homewood, IL: Dow Jones-Irwin, 1987).

19. Harris, T.A. *I'm OK, You're OK* (London: Pan, 1967).

20. Guirdham, M. *Interpersonal Skills At Work* (Hemel Hempstead, Hertfordshire: Prentice Hall, 1990) p 123.

21. Ibid., p 19.

22. Ibid., pp 123–126.

23. Ibid.

24. Goffman, *The Presentation of Self in Everyday Life*, p 25.

25. Ibid., p 15.

26. Ibid., pp 20–21.

27. Ibid., pp 222–230.

28. Brown, *Richard Branson: The Inside Story*, pp 140-141.

29. Goffman, E. *Interaction Ritual: Essays on Face-to-Face Behaviour* (London: Penguin Books, 1972).

30. Stevens, M. *Sudden Death: The Rise and Fall of E.F. Hutton* (New York: Penguin, 1989) pp 82–83. Reprinted by permission of Dominick Abel Literary Agency. Copyright © 1989 Mark Stevens. First published by Dutton Signet.

31. Greenslade, R. *Maxwell's Fall* (London: Simon and Schuster Ltd, 1992) p 33. From "Maxwell: The Rise and Fall of Robert Maxwell and His Empire" by Roy Greenslade. Copyright © 1992 by Roy

Greenslade. Published by arrangement with Carol Publishing Group. A Birch Lane Press Book. Reprinted by permission of Simon and Schuster.

32. Pfeffer, *Managing With Power: Politics and Influence in Organizations*, pp 168–171.

33. Caro, R. *Means of Ascent: The Years of Lyndon Johnson* (New York: Alfred A. Knopf, 1990).

34. Kotter, J.P. *The General Managers* (New York: The Free Press, 1982) p 46.

35. Pfeffer, *Managing With Power: Politics and Influence in Organizations*, p 176.

36. Puzo, M. *The Godfather* (London: Heinemann, 1974).

37. Brown, *Richard Branson: The Inside Story*, pp 229–230.

38. Ibid.

39. Christie, R. & Geis, F.L. *Studies in Machiavellianism* (New York: Academic Press, 1970) p 312. Reprinted by permission of the Academic Press, Inc, and the authors' representative.

40. Pfeffer, *Managing With Power: Politics and Influence in Organizations*, p 170.

41. Barry, J.M. *The Ambition and the Power* (New York: Viking, 1989) p 20. Reprinted by permission of the author and the Sagalyn Agency.

42. Slatter, S. *Corporate Recovery: A Guide to Turnaround Management* (London: Penguin Books, 1987) pp 121, 319.

43. Jennings, R., Cox, C. & Cooper, G.L. *Business Elites: The Psychology of Entrepreneurs and Intrapreneurs* (London: Routledge, 1994) p 37. Reprinted by permission of International Thomson Publishing Services.

44. Smith, D.K. & Alexander, R.C. *Fumbling the Future: How Xerox Invented, Then Ignored, the First Personal Computer* (New York: William Morrow, 1988) p 131. Used by permission of William Morrow & Co. Inc. © 1988 by Robert C. Alexander and Douglas K. Smith.

45. Ibid.

46. Pfeffer, *Managing With Power: Politics and Influence in Organizations*, pp 174–175.

47. Kanter, M.R. *The Change Masters: Corporate Entrepreneurs at Work* (London: Allen & Unwin, 1984).

48. Pfeffer, *Managing With Power: Politics and Influence in Organizations*, pp 182–183.

49. Dobbs, M. *House of Cards* (London: Harper Collins, 1993).

50. Thatcher, M. *Margaret Thatcher, The Downing Street Years* (Harper Collins, 1993) pp 757–758. Reprinted by permission of Harper Collins Publishers Limited.

51. Pfeffer, *Managing With Power: Politics and Influence in Organizations*, pp 166–167.

52. Kotter, *The General Managers*, p 19.

53. Thomson, *Margaret Thatcher: The Woman Within*, p 115.

54. Jennings, Cox, & Cooper, *Business Elites*, pp 106–107.

55. Smith, S.B. *In all his Glory: The Life of William S. Paley* (New York: Simon and Schuster, 1990) p 394. Reprinted with the permission of Simon and Schuster from *In All His Glory: The Life of William S. Paley* by Sally Bedell Smith. Copyright © 1990 by Sally Bedell Smith.

56. Brown, *Richard Branson: The Inside Story*, p 137.

chapter four

1. Gardner, J.W. *On Leadership* (New York: Free Press, 1990) pp 50–51. Copyright © 1990 by John W. Gardner, Inc. Reprinted with the permission of the Free Press, a Division of Simon and Schuster, and Sterling Lord Literistic, Inc.

2. Clancy, P. & Elder, S. *TIP: A Biography of Thomas P. O'Neill, Speaker of the House* (New York: Macmillan, 1980) p 4. Reprinted with the permisson of Simon & Schuster from *TIP: A Biography of Thomas P. O'Neill, Speaker of the House* by Paul R. Clancy and Shirley Elder. Copyright © 1980 by Paul R. Clancy and Shirley Elder.

3. Smith, B.S. *In all his Glory: The Life of William S. Paley* (New York: Simon & Schuster, 1990) p 404. Reprinted with the permission of Simon and Schuster. Copyright © 1990 by Sally Bedell Smith.

4. Ibid.

5. Heller, F.A. & Porter, L.W. "Personal Characteristics Conducive to Job Success in Business", *The Manager*, Jan./Feb. 1966.

6. Fiedler, F.E. "A Contingency Model of Leadership Effectiveness" in Berkowitz, L. (ed.), *Advances in Experiential Social Psychology*, Vol. 1 (New York: Academic Press, 1964) pp 150–191.

7. Bower, T. *Tiny Rowland, A Rebel Tycoon* (London: Manderin, 1994) p 33. Reprinted by the permission of Curtis Brown on behalf of Tom Bower. Copyright © Tom Bower 1994.

8. Ratui, I. "Thinking Internationally: A Comparison of How International Executives Learn," *International Studies of Management and Organisation*, Vol. XIII, No. 1-2 (Spring–Summer 1983), pp 139–150.

9. Jones, E.E. & Nisbett, R.E. *The Actor and the Observer: Divergent Perceptions of the Causes of Behavior* (New York: General Learning Press, 1971).

10. Kelley, Harold H. "The Process of Casual Attribution," *American Psychologist*, (1973) pp 107–128.

11. Kolb, D.A., Rubin, M.I. & McIntyre, J.M. *Organizational Psychology – An Experiential Approach* (Englewood Cliffs, NJ: Prentice Hall, 1971).

12. Bower, *Tiny Rowland, A Rebel Tycoon*, pp 606–607.

13. Ibid., p 607.

14. Ibid., p 608.

15. Burger, P. & Bass, B.M. *Assessment of Managers: An International Comparison* (New York: Free Press, 1979).

16. Warr, P.B. & Knapper, C.K. *The Perception of People and Events* (London: Wiley, 1968).

17. Thatcher, M. *Margaret Thatcher, The Downing Street Years* (London: Harper Collins, 1993) pp 310–311. Reprinted with permission of Harper Collins Publishers Limited.

18. Cohen, A.R. & Bradford, D.L. *Influence without Authority* (New York: John Wiley and Sons, 1990) pp 101–120.

19. Ekman, P. & Friesen, W.V. "Non-Verbal Behavior in Psychotherapy Research" in Schlien, J.M. (ed.), *Research in Psychotherapy*, Washington DC: American Psychological Association, Vol.3 (1968).

20. Argyle, M., Ingham, R., Aikens, F., & McCallin, M. "The Different Functions of Gaze," *Semiotica*, 1 (1973), pp 19–32.

21. Knapp, M.L. *Nonverbal Communication in Human Interaction*, (2nd edn) (New York: Holt, Rhinehart and Winston, 1978) pp 132–133.

22. Exline, R.V. "Visual Interaction: The Glances of Power and Preference," in Cole, J.K. (ed.), *Nebraska Symposium on Motivation*, Vol. 19 (Lincoln: University of Nebraska Press, 1971).

23. Thomson, A., *Margaret Thatcher: The Woman Within* (London: W.H. Allen, 1989) p 48. Reprinted with permission of the Sharland Organisation and the author Andrew Thomson.

24. Major, B. & Heslin, R. *Perceptions of Same-sex and Cross-sex*

Touching: It's Better to Give Than to Receive. Paper presented at meeting of Midwestern Psychological Association, Chicago, May 1978.

25. Thomson, *Margaret Thatcher: The Woman Within*, p 49.

26. Hall, E. (1966) *The Hidden Dimension* and (1959) *The Silent Language* (New York: Doubleday).

27. Brown, *Richard Branson: The Inside Story* (Headline Book Publishing, 1994) p 239. Reprinted by permission of the Peters Fraser & Dunlop Group Ltd.

28. Chippendale, P. & Horrie, C. *Stick It Up Your Punter: the Rise and Fall of the Sun* (London: Heinemann, 1990) pp 89–90. Reprinted by permission of the Peters Fraser & Dunlop Group Ltd and Reed Books.

29. Ibid., p 90.

30. Ibid., p 89.

31. Ibid., p 94.

32. Knapp, *Nonverbal Communication in Human Interaction*, (2nd edn), pp 147–172.

33. Chippendale & Horrie, *Stick it up your Punter*, p 90.

34. Thomson, *Margaret Thatcher: The Woman Within*, pp 223–224.

35. Cohen & Bradford, *Influence without Authority*, pp 105–108.

chapter five

1. Peters, T. "Connectors Help: Don't Fear Them" from his "Peters on Excellence" column, *Union News*, Springfield, MA, 8 Sept. 1992, pp 1, 19.

2. Kotter, J.P. *The General Managers* (New York: Free Press, 1982) p 67.

3. Pace, R.W. *Organizational Communication: Foundations for Human Resource Development* (New York: Prentice Hall, 1983).

4. Deal, T.E. & Kennedy, A.A. *Corporate Cultures: The Rites and Rituals of Corporate Life* (Reading, MA: Addison-Wesley Publishing Company, 1983) p 41. © 1982 by Addison-Wesley Publishing Company, Inc. Reprinted by permission of Addison-Wesley Longman Publishing Company, Inc. and Penguin Books, 1988.

5. Ibid., p 143.

6. Kanter, M.E. *When Giants Learn To Dance* (London: Unwin Hyman, 1989). Reprinted with the permission of Simon and Schuster. Copyright © 1989 by Rosabeth Moss Kanter.

7. Ibid., p 361.

8. Based on General Electric Annual Report, 1989.

9. Pettigrew, A.M. "On Studying Organisational Culture," *Administrative Science Quarterly*, Dec. 1979, pp 570-581.

10. Kakabadse, A., Ludlow, R. & Vinnicombe, S. *Working in Organisations* (London: Penguin, 1985) pp 226–227.

11. Handy, C. *Understanding Organisations* (London: Penguin Books, 1985) pp 186–187. Reprinted by permission of Penguin Books Ltd. Copyright © Charles Handy, 1976, 1981, 1985.

12. Deal & Kennedy, *Corporate Cultures*, p 17.

13. Handy, *Understanding Organisations*, p 188.

14. Deal & Kennedy, *Corporate Cultures*, p 11.

15. Knowlton, C. "How Disney Keeps the Magic Going," *Fortune*, 4 Dec. 1989, pp 111–132.

16. Deal & Kennedy, *Corporate Cultures*, pp 32–33.

17. Ibid., p 193.

18. Harrison, R. "How to Describe Your Organization," *Harvard Business Review*, Sept./Oct. 1972.

19. Chippendale, P. & Horrie, C. *Stick It Up Your Punter: The Rise and Fall of the Sun* (London: William Heinemann, 1990) p 328. Reprinted by permission of the Peters Fraser & Dunlop Group Ltd and Reed Books.

20. Brummer, A. & Cowe, R. *Hanson: The Rise and Rise of Britain's Most Buccaneering Businessman* (London: Fourth Estate, 1994) p 7.

21. Sampson, A. *The Sovereign State of ITT* (Briarcliff Manor, NY: Stein and Day, 1980) pp 95–97.

22. Robins, S.P. *Management* (4th edn) (Englewood Cliffs, NJ: Prentice Hall, 1984) pp 90–91.

23. "Who's Afraid of IBM?" *Business Week*, 29 June 1987, p 72. Reprinted by permission of Business Week.

24. Ibid.

25. Deal & Kennedy, *Corporate Cultures*, pp 129-139.

26. Wright, J.P. *On a Clear Day You Can See General Motors* (Grosse Point, MI: Wright Enterprises, 1979) p 41.

27. Andrews, E.L. "Out of Chaos," *Business Month*, Dec. 1989, p 33. No trace.

28. Deal & Kennedy, *Corporate Cultures*, p 135.

29. Ibid., p 53.

30. Neustadt, R. *Presidential Power* (New York: Wiley, 1960). © 1960.

Reprinted with permission of Allyn and Bacon. All rights reserved.

31. Luthans, F., Hodgetts, R.M. & Rosenkrantz, S.A. *Real Managers* (Cambridge, MA: Ballinger Publishing Company, 1988).

32. Ibid., p 72.

33. Mintzberg, H. (1990) "The Manager's Job: Folklore and Fact" in J. Gabarro (ed.) *Managing People and Organizations* (Boston, MA: Harvard Business School Publications, 1992).

34. Rose, F. *West of Eden: The End of Innocence at Apple Computer* (New York: Viking Penguin, 1989) p 298. Copyright © 1989 by Frank Rose. Used by permission of Viking Penguin, a division of Penguin Books USA Inc., and International Creative Management.

35. Ibid.

36. Kaplan, R.E. "Trade Routes: The Manager's Network of Relationships," *Organizational Dynamics*, Spring 1984, p 41. © 1984. Reprinted by permission of the American Management Association, New York. All rights reserved.

37. Kotter, J. *The General Managers*, p 67.

38. Raelin, J.A. *The Clash of Cultures: Managers Managing Professionals* (Boston, MA: Harvard Business School Press, 1991) p 137.

39. Shea, M. *Influence: How to Make the System Work for You* (London: Century Hutchinson, 1988) p 4.

40. Caro, R.A. *The Path to Power: The Years of Lyndon Johnson* (New York: Alfred A. Knopf, 1982) p 226. Reprinted by permission of Random House, Inc.

41. Savage, C.M. *Fifth Generation Management: Integrating Enterprises through Human Networking* (Oxford, Heinemann, 1996).

42. Critchley, J. *Michael Heseltine* (London: André Deutsch, 1987) pp 36–37. Reprinted by permission of André Deutsch Ltd and Curtis Brown Ltd, London on behalf of Julian Critchley. Copyright © Julian Critchley 1987.

43. Cohen, R.A. & Bradford, D.L. "Influence Without Authority: The Use of Alliances, Reciprocity, and Exchange to Accomplish Work," *Organizational Dynamics*, Winter 1989, pp 5–17.

44. Levinson, H. & Rosenthal, S. *CEO: Corporate Leadership in Action* (New York: Basic Books, 1984) p 68. Reprinted with the permission of Harper Collins Publishers Inc. Copyright © 1985 by Harry Levison and Stuart Rosenthal.

45. Quickel, S.W. "Welch on Welch, CEO of the Year," *Financial World*, 3 April 1990, pp 62–67.

46. Critchley, J. *Michael Heseltine*, p 37.
47. Deal & Kennedy, *Corporate Cultures*, p 91.
48. Shea, *Influence*, p 52.

chapter six

1. Yukl, G. & Falbe, C.M. "Influence Tactics and Objectives in Upward, Downward, and Lateral Influence Attempts," *Journal of Applied Psychology*, Vol. 75, No. 2 (1990), pp 132–140.
2. Ibid., p 133.
3. Kipnis, D. & Schmidt, S.M. "Intraorganizational Influence Tactics: Explorations in Getting One's Way," *Journal of Applied Psychology*, Vol. 65, No. 4 (1980), p 445.
4. Chippendale, P. & Horrie, C. *Stick It Up Your Punter: The Rise and Fall of the Sun* (London: Heinemann, 1990) p 85. Reprinted by permission of the Peters Fraser and Dunlop Group Ltd and Reed Books.
5. Ibid., pp 89–92.
6. Bernoth, A. "Sugar takes reins to spur fresh revival," *The Sunday Times*, 31 Dec. 1995. © Times Newspapers Limited, 1995.
7. Burrough, B. & Helyar, J. *Barbarians at the Gate: The Rise and Fall of RJR Nabisco* (New York: Harper and Row, 1990) p 24. Reprinted by permission of Harper Collins Publishers. Copyright © 1990 by Bryan Burrough and John Helyar.
8. Yukl & Falbe, "Influence Tactics and Objectives," p 133.
9. Kipnis & Schmidt, "Intraorganizational Influence Tactics," p 446.
10. Kotter, J. *The General Managers* (New York: The Free Press, 1982) p 73.
11. Yukl & Falbe, "Influence Tactics and Objectives," p 133.
12. Gouldner, A. "The Norm of Reciprocity: A Preliminary Statement," *American Sociological Review*, 25 (1960), pp 161–178.
13. Kotter, *The General Managers*, pp 69,72.
14. Burrough & Helyar, *Barbarians at the Gate*, pp 33–37
15. Brummer, A. & Cowe, R. *Hanson: The Rise and Rise of Britain's Most Buccaneering Businessman* (London: Fourth Estate, 1995) pp 5, 6, 180.
16. Yukl & Falbe, "Influence Tactics and Objectives," p 133.
17. Pfeffer, J. *Managing with Power: Politics and Influence in Organizations* (Boston, MA: Harvard Business School Press, 1992) p 83. Reprinted by permission of Harvard Business School Press. Copy-

right © 1992 by the President and Fellows of Harvard College, all rights reserved.

18. Chippendale & Horrie, *Stick It Up Your Punter*, p 94.

19. Hersh, S.M. *The Price of Power: Kissinger in the Nixon White House* (New York: Summit Books, 1983) p 24.

20. Yukl & Falbe, "Influence Tactics and Objectives," p 133.

21. Kipnis & Schmidt, "Intraorganizational Influence Tactics," p 445.

22. Thomson, A *Margaret Thatcher: The Woman Within* (London: W. H. Allen, 1989) p 140. Reprinted by permission of the Sharland Organisation and the author Andrew Thomson.

23. Bower, T. *Tiny Rowland: A Rebel Tycoon* (London: William Heinemann, 1993) p 413. Reprinted by permission of Curtis Brown on behalf of Tom Bower. Copyright © Tom Bower 1994.

24. Ibid., p 74.

25. Ibid., p 77.

26. Rose, F. *West of Eden: The End of Innocence at Apple Computers* (New York: Viking Penguin, 1989) p 276. Copyright © 1989 by Frank Rose. Used by permission of Viking Penguin, a division of Penguin Books USA Inc., and International Creative Management.

27. Ibid.

28. Yukl & Falbe, "Influence Tactics and Objectives," p 133.

29. Kipnis & Schmidt, "Intraorganizational Influence Tactics," p 445.

30. Keys, B. & Case, T. "How to become an Influential Manager," *Academy of Management Executive*, Vol. 4, No. 4 (1990), p 41. Reprinted by permission of Academy of Management.

31. Thomson, A. *Margaret Thatcher: The Woman Within*, p 135.

32. Smith Bedell, S. *In All His Glory: The Life of William S. Paley* (New York: Simon and Schuster, 1990) p 152. Reprinted with permission of Simon & Schuster. Copyright © 1990 by Sally Bedell Smith.

33. Ibid.

34. Yukl & Falbe, "Influence Tactics and Objectives," p 133.

35. John F. Kennedy's Inaugural Address, 20 January 1961.

36. Brown, M. *Richard Branson: The Inside Story* (London: Headline Book Publishing, 1994) pp 213–214. Reprinted by permission of the Peters Fraser & Dunlop Group Ltd.

37. Ibid., p 215.

38. Milene Henley, F. "Good, Better, Best," *Working Women*, Dec. 1987, pp 86–89. Reprinted by permission of Working Women Magazine. Copyright © 1987 by Working Women Magazine.

39. Pfeffer, *Managing with Power: Politics and Influence in Organizations*, p 279.
40. Ibid.
41. Yukl & Falbe, "Influence Tactics and Objectives," p 133.
42. Tichy, N.M. & Charan, R. "The CEO As Coach: An Interview with Allied Signal's Lawrence A. Bossidy," *Harvard Business Review*, March–April 1995, pp 70, 77, 78. Reprinted by permission of Harvard Business Review. Copyright © 1995 by the President and Fellows of Harvard College, all rights reserved.
43. Yukl & Falbe, "Influence Tactics and Objectives," p 134.
44. Ibid.
45. Keys, B. & Case, T. "How to become an Influential Manager," *Academy of Management Executive*, Vol. 4, No. 4 (1990), p 44.
46. Ibid., p 47.
47. Kotter, J.P. *The Leadership Factor* (New York: The Free Press, 1988) p 18. Copyright © 1988 by John P. Kotter, Inc. Reprinted with the permisison of The Free Press, a Division of Simon & Schuster.
48. Yukl & Falbe, "Influence Tactics and Objectives," p 132.
49. Keys & Case, "How to become an Influential Manager," p 46.
50. Stewart, T.A. "GE Keeps Those Ideas Coming," *Fortune*, Aug. 1991, pp 12, 23. Reprinted by permission of Fortune Magazine.
51. Tichy, N.M. & Charan, R., *Harvard Business Review*, Sept.–Oct. 1989.
52. Bartlett, C.A. & Ghoshal, S., "Changing the Role of Top Management Beyond Systems to People," *Harvard Business Review*, Jan.–Feb. 1995, p 140.
53. Ibid.
54. Handy, C. *Understanding Organisations* (London: Penguin, 3rd edn, 1985) pp 138–142. Reproduced by permission of Penguin Books Ltd. Copyright © Charles B. Handy, 1976, 1981, 1985.
55. Stewart, T.A. "GE Keeps Those Ideas Coming," p 23.
56. Handy, *Understanding Organisations*, p 142.
57. Kissinger, H. *The White House Years* (Boston, MA: Little Brown, 1979) p 39.

chapter seven

1. Wansell, G. *Tycoon: The Life of James Goldsmith* (London: Grafton Books, 1987) p 341. Reprinted by permission of Harper Collins Publishers and the author's agent John Johnson.

2. Pfeffer, J., *Managing with Power: Politics and Influence in Organizations* (Boston, MA: Harvard Business School Press, 1992) p 344. Reprinted by permission of Harvard Business School Press. Copyright © 1992 by the President and Fellows of Harvard College, all rights reserved.

3. Johnson, D.W. & Johnson, F.P. *Joining Together: Group Theory and Group Skills* (Englewood Cliffs, NJ: Prentice Hall, 1975).

4. Dreyfus, H.L., Dreyfus, S.E., & Athanasion, T. *Mind over Machine: The Power of Human Intuition and Expertise in the Era of the Computer* (New York: The Free Press, 1986).

5. Rose, F. *West of Eden: The End of Innocence at Apple Computer* (New York: Viking Penguin, 1989) p 78. Copyright © 1989 by Frank Rose. Used by permission of Viking Penguin, a division of Penguin Books USA Inc., and International Creative Management.

6. Ibid.

7. Stewart, T.A. "GE Keeps Those Ideas Coming," *Fortune*, Aug. 1991, pp 12, 23.

8. Thomson, A. *Margaret Thatcher: The Woman Within* (London: W.H. Allen, 1989) p 25. Reprinted by permission of the Sharland Organisation and the author, Andrew Thomson.

9. Handy, C. *The Age of Unreason* (London: Business Books Ltd, 1989) p 181.

10. Kennedy, J.F., Extract from his inaugural address as President of the USA on January 20, 1961.

index